NĀGĀRJUNA'S LETTER
to
King Gautamīputra

Known in Tibetan as

SLOB. DPON. KLU. SGRUB. KYI. BSHES. ṖA'I.
SPRINGS. YIG.

Known in Sanskrit as

SUHṚLLEKHA

NĀGĀRJUNA'S LETTER
to
King Gautamīputra

With Explanatory Notes
Based on Tibetan Commentaries
and

A Preface by His Holiness Sakya Trizin

Translated into English from the Tibetan by

VENERABLE LOZANG JAMSPAL
VENERABLE NGAWANG SAMTEN CHOPHEL
PETER DELLA SANTINA

MOTILAL BANARSIDASS PUBLISHERS
PRIVATE LIMITED • DELHI

Reprint: Delhi, 1983, 1996, 2004, 2008
First Edition: Delhi, 1978

ISBN : 978-81-208-1375-5

MOTILAL BANARSIDASS
41 U.A. Bungalow Road, Jawahar Nagar, Delhi 110 007
8 Mahalaxmi Chamber, 22 Bhulabhai Desai Road, Mumbai 400 026
203 Royapettah High Road, Mylapore, Chennai 600 004
236, 9th Main III Block, Jayanagar, Bangalore 560 011
Sanas Plaza, 1302 Baji Rao Road, Pune 411 002
8 Camac Street, Kolkata 700 017
Ashok Rajpath, Patna 800 004
Chowk, Varanasi 221 001

PRINTED IN INDIA

By Jainendra Prakash Jain at Shri Jainendra Press,
A-45, Naraina, Phase-I, New Delhi 110 028
and Published by Narendra Prakash Jain for
Motilal Banarsidass Publishers Private Limited,
Bungalow Road, Delhi 110 007

This work is dedicated to

His Holiness the Sakya Trizin,
Ngawang Kunga Thegchen Palbar Thinley Samphel
Wang Gi Gyalpo

through whose kindness the great bliss itself arises
in an instant—

Your voice, compassionate lord,
spreads to all the directions the joy arising
from the truth of the Mahāyāna Path.

Auspicious signs foretelling the blossoming
of happiness for all living beings are
Your transcendental actions.

Wishing to increase the knowledge of those deluded,
the real nature of all things is revealed
by the power of Your mind.

O King of Dharma,
who are a refuge for those in need—
bestow blessings upon all the world.

PREFACE

His Holiness
Sakya Trizin
HEAD OF THE SAKYAPA SECT
OF TIBETAN BUDDHISM

Rajpur,
Dehra Dun,
India,
September 20,1975

The <u>Letter Of A Friend</u> of Arya Nagarjuna has been held in high esteem by Tibetans throughout the centuries as a fundamental text for those embarking on the Path of Dharma. For this reason, I am extremely pleased to see this publication of its English translation which will enable the many Westerners who have become interested in the Buddha's Dharma to read and study its important teaching. Through the comprehension and application of its instructions, one will be able to place his feet firmly on the path leading to liberation just as an elephant firmly plants his feet on the ground as he walks.

In one way, <u>The Letter Of A Friend</u> may be viewed as consisting of two divisions. The first is the accumulation of merit which here is the path of moral discipline, study and meditation which leads one away from 1) desire for this life, and 2) desire for Saṁsāra as a whole. The second is the accumulation of wisdom which here is the realization of Lord Buddha's profound and precious doctrine of Interdependent Origination which leads one to the final enlightenment of a Buddha.

Moral discipline, the acceptance and observance of various vows, serves as the very foundation for all subsequent achievements. Study enables one to take hold of the bright lamp of knowledge which dispels ignorance and wrong views and allows one to acquire the wisdom necessary to traverse the path to liberation. Meditation calms the mind, produces the correctives for removing the defilements and establishes the foundation of mindfulness which leads one to understand impermanence, suffering, selflessness, and emptiness.

Having acquired these requisites, one is then in a position to begin his quest for transcendental knowledge. Armed with the weapon of Interdependent Origination, the mighty sword of emptiness, one is able to vanquish the ignorance that veils the truth —— just as Lord Buddha did under the Bodhi tree two thousand five hundred and nineteen years ago.

Both of these accumulations are necessary for attaining liberation, just as it is necessary for a bird to have two wings to soar high in the sky. Thus, if one follows the advice given by the great saint Nagarjuna in this letter, one will also gain supreme enlightenment like the Buddha Shākyamuni.

Sakya Trizin

Sakya Trizin

CONTENTS

LIST OF ILLUSTRATIONS

FOREWORD

The work contained herein is a compilation of a translation of the root verses of *Nāgārjuna's Letter to King Gautamīputra* along with explanatory notes which are based upon three commentaries of *Nāgārjuna's Letter to King Gautamīputra* written by Jetsun Rendawa Shonnu Lodo, the Venerable Lozang Jinpa and the Venerable Rongton Sheja Kunrig. Jetsun Rendawa Shonnu Lodo (1349-1412) was a famed scholar of the Sakya sect and was one of the teachers of the Reverend Je Tsongkhapa. His commentary of Ācārya Nāgārjuna's *Suhṛllekha*, bshes. pa'i. springs.yig.gi. 'grel.pa.don.gsal.bzhugs.so., is held by most Tibetan scholars to be one of the most authoritative. Bshes. pa'i.springs. yig. gi. rnam. bshad. 'phags. pa'i. dgongs.pa.kun. gsal. zhes.bya. ba. bzhugs.so., the commentry of the Venerable Lozang Jinpa, a monk of the Gelugpa sect who resided at Tashi Lhunpo Monastery, was relied upon heavily. In fact, Lobsang Jinpa's commentary is based upon that of Jetsun Rendawa's. The third commentary, legs.par bshes.pa'i.springs. yig.gi.rnam.bshad.thar.lam.bde.ba'i. them.skas zhes.bya.ba., used mostly for clarification on various points, was written by the Venerable Rongton Sheja Kunrig (1367-1449), a renowned scholar of the Sakya sect and founder of the Nālandā Monastery in Tibet.

The explanatory notes which serve as the commentary for this text are not direct translations of any of the three Tibetan commentaries mentioned above, but summaries of their contents as explained by His Holiness Sakya Trizin. These notes were taken during a number of sessions and later rewritten for the purpose of clarifying the import of the verses. The outline within which the verses and commentary are presented is a translation of the one used in the commentary of Jetsun Rendawa.

The Sanskrit text of the *Suhṛllekha* is no longer extant. However, there exist various editions of its Tibetan translation, three translations into Chinese and three earlier translations into

English.* The Tibetan text here employed was published by A.Sonam in Varanasi, India, 1971, under the title, slob.dpon.klu. sgrub.kyi. bshes.pa'i.springs.yig.dang.de'i.rnam.bshad.dge.bshes. blo.bzang.sbyin.pas.mdzad.pa.bcas.bzhugs.so. This edition of the *Suhṛllekha* was translated into Tibetan by the Indian Abbot Sarvajñadeva and the Tibetan redactor-translator Vande. dpal. brtsegs.

We are greatly indebted to His Holiness Sakya Trizin for the invaluable guidance bestowed upon us in this and all other works. Deep gratitude is due to Khenpo Appey Rinpoche, principal of the Sakya College, for explanation of the true import, and clarification of various points, of this work. Also, sincere thanks are due to the Venerable Nima Sangpo of the Sakya College for his help in translating the various verses found in our commentary. Special acknowledgement and thanks are due to Rinzing Lhadipa Lama of Chungyal House, Gangtok, Sikkim, for his contribution of the drawings found herein. Finally, we wish to acknowledge Sonam Basgo Tongpon for the calligraphy of the Tibetan text and N. Sonam Tenzin for his unfailing encouragement.

It is our sincere prayer that this work will be instrumental in placing all others on the path of Dharma.

September, 1975
Dehra Dun, India

TRANSLATORS

*Dr. Wenzel translated the *Suhṛllekha* from Tibetan: *Nāgārjuna's Friendly Epistle*, Journal of the Pali Text Society, 1886, pp.6-32. S. Beale translated the *Suhṛllekha* from Chinese: see *Indian Antiquity*, 1887, pp. 169 ff. The Venerable Bhikkhu Khantipalo translated the *Suhṛllekha* from Tibetan: *The Letter of Kind-heartedness of Acārya Nāgārjuna* in *The Wisdom Gone Beyond*, pp. 13-44, Bankok, 1966.

The two earlier translations were done at a time when the study of Mahāyāna Buddhism was in its infancy, and so they lack a proper understanding of the content and significance of the work. The latter translation though exhibiting an appreciation of the subject matter and poetic skill, strays from the meaning of the original in numerous places.

INTRODUCTION

Ācārya Nāgārjuna holds an almost unequalled place among the ranks of those Buddhist saints who expounded the teaching of the Buddha Śākyamuni for the benefit of the world. As prophesied in the *Laṅkāvatāra Sūtra*, the *Mañjuśrīmūlakalpa Tantra*, as well as in several other discourses of the Buddha, Ācārya Nāgārjuna revolutionized the interpretation of the doctrine of the Enlightened One which was current at his time and lent it a vitality and dynamism which has continued to sustain it even to our day among the votaries of the Mahāyāna. The revolution which Ācārya Nāgārjuna accomplished within the fold of Buddhism was not, as some might think, a radical departure from the original doctrine of the Buddha Śākyamuni. On the contrary, the adherents of the Madhyamaka school are undoubtedly justified in asserting that their interpretation represents the true import of the doctrine of the Buddha and the essence of Buddhism. Although it is not our purpose here to substantiate this claim, it may simply be said that its truth has not escaped the notice of competent scholars in the field.

Given the majesty of Ācārya Nāgārjuna's name and the importance of the role which he played in the development of Buddhist thought, it is not surprising that the story of his life and achievements, as traditionally told, should partake of the fabulous and the legendary. In recounting the life of the Ācārya, his biographers have invariably included elements which, though undoubtedly facts of religious history, are difficult to establish in actuality. While an English translation of one of the many biographies of Ācārya Nāgārjuna which are extant in the Tibetan language is certainly desirable, it is a task of no small magnitude. Hence for the purpose of introduction to this present work we have chosen to confine ourselves to a brief account of the life of the Ācārya based upon facts which can be established with relative certainty, drawing upon the accounts of the traditional biographers only in so far as they do not contradict these facts.

Ācārya Nāgārjuna lived sometime during the last quarter of

the first century C.E. and the first quarter of the second century C.E. This is evident from his acknowledged friendship with a king of the Śātavāhana line of Āndhra. The king, Gautamīputra Śātakarṇi, son of queen Bala Śrī, was the only one of his line to embrace Buddhism, and it was for him that Ācārya Nāgāijuna wrote the *Suhṛllekha* and *Ratnāvalī*. That the king in question reigned at about the time indicated is certain from the evidence of present archaeological discoveries.* The traditional biographers agree that the Ācārya was born in a *brahmin* family of South India. The Tibetan accounts state that at his birth, astrologers prophesied that the child would not live beyond the age of seven. Unable to bear the sight of his premature death, the accounts tell us, his parents sent the boy to a Buddhist monastery, where — by reciting the *Aparimitāyudhāraṇī* — he succeeded in escaping his fate. The account given by Kumārajīva of Ācārya Nāgārjuna's early life differ ssubstantially from that of the Tibetan biographers. It is mentioned here only because it is presumably earlier than the latter, and so perhaps deserves consideration. Kumārajīva writes that in his youth Ācārya Nāgārjuna was overcome with lust and through the art of invisibility seduced women in the royal palace. Once, however, he narrowly escaped death at the hands of the guards, an experience which led him to dwell upon the Buddha's teaching that desire is the foremost cause of suffering. As a result, according to Kumārajīva, the Ācārya entered the Buddhist Order. Thereafter, the Tibetan accounts state, Nāgārjuna became a student of Rāhulabhadra† who was then the abbot of the great university at Nālandā.

Virtually all the traditional biographers agree that Ācārya Nāgārjuna procured some *Prajñāpāramitā Sūtras* from the Nāgas. Though some have suggested that this term may have been used to indicate a band of great *yogis*, the exact significance of the reference remains uncertain. Finally, Ācārya Nāgārjuna seems to have spent the latter part of his life at the monastery built for him by his

*See *Nāgārjuna's Philosophy* by K. V. Ramanan, Bharatiya Vidya Prakashan, Varanasi, India, 1971, p.25.

†Rāhulabhadra is also known as the Mahāsiddha Sarāha.

friend and patron, King Gautamīputra at Śrī Parvata. Although the accounts given of the manner of the Ācarya's death differ with regard to detail, they agree in that Nāgārjuna consented to his own death at the hands of the son of King Gautamīputra.

Ācarya Nāgārjuna was an accomplished master of Buddhist doctrine. He wrote voluminously on almost every aspect of Buddhist philosophy and religion. Although Ācarya Nāgārjuna has rightly won widespread acclaim as the foremost exponent of the 'middle way', or *Madhyamāpratipad*, and as a master of dialectic, his writings also include works on *Vinaya*, on *Tantra*, on the career of the Bodhisattva, and on the practice of the *Pāramitāyāna*. Among the latter are counted his commentary on the *Daśabhūmikāsūtra*, the *Sūtrasamuccaya* and others. Ācarya Nāgārjuna also wrote works of a highly devotional character, such as the *Catuḥstava*. It is lamentable that thus far so few of the writings of the Ācarya have been made available in English translation. It is hoped that in the years to come this situation may be remedied and that the publication of this short work of Nāgārjuna's in English may contribute in a small degree to that process.

The *Suhṛllekha* of Ācarya Nāgārjuna is a concise and comprehensive summary of Buddhist teaching. It can generally be said to belong to a class of texts which later came to be called, in Tibet, those of the graduated path or *lam.rim.* The works of Nāgārjuna, most especially the *Sūtrasamuccaya* but also to a lesser degree the *Suhṛllekha*, were the forerunners of a multitude of texts which can be classed under the name *lam.rim.* They include such works as the *Śikṣāsamuccaya* of Śāntideva, *The Jewel Ornament of Liberation* of Sgam.po.pa. and the *Clarification Of The Thought Of The Sage* of the Sakya Paṇḍita Kunga. Gyaltsen. Pal. Zangpo. It is not surprising that the concise style and comprehensive content of a work like Nāgārjuna's *Suhṛllekha* should have rendered it so popular as a vehicle for conveying in brief the teaching of Buddhism. That the *Suhṛllekha* enjoyed such popularity even in India is evident from the account of the Chinese pilgrim I-Tsing who visited India in the 7th century, for he writes, "In India students learn this epistle in verse early in the course of instruction, but the most devout make it their special object of study throughout their lives."* Today, also, the *Suhṛllekha* enjoys widespread popularity among Tibetans who use it with regularity as a basic manual for teaching Buddhist Dharma. Hence it may be ventured that its translation in English will prove useful for those who wish to acquire a fundamental grasp of Buddhist Religion. The comprehensive character of the work, though short, renders it highly suitable for use as an introduction to the whole of Buddhism. As it was written principally for laymen, addressed as it was to the Śātavāhana king with whom Nāgārjuna shared a lifelong friendship, the teachings it encompasses can be appreciated by a wide spectrum of readers with varying interests. Though scholars and academicians seeking clarification of abstruse points of the doctrine of the Mādhyamikas may find little to satisfy them in the *Suhṛllekha*, those who desire a concise and comprehensive manual of instruction in the doctrine and practice of Buddhist philosophy and religion will surely not be disappointed.

Though the *Suhṛllekha* contains elements which belong specifically to the Mahāyāna, much of its content comprises a common foundation which both the Hīnayāna and Mahāyāna share. The letter commences with an invocation to cultivate faith in that which is preeminent and exalted, such as the Buddha, Dharma and Saṅgha. There follows a lengthy summary of ethical and religious precepts which, if adhered to, result in birth in the fortunate realms of men and gods, as Ācārya Nāgārjuna writes, "...morality is said to be the foundation of all virtues, just as the earth is (the support of both) animate and inanimate things". The injunctions and prohibitions set forth in the text are accompanied by practices which are to be employed to counteract non-virtuous propensities. As Ārya Nāgārjuna says in the fortieth verse, "Always meditate rightly on love, compassion, joy and equanimity...". Of equal im-

**A Record Of The Buddhist Religion As Practised In India and the Malay Archipelago* (*A.D.*671-695) by I-Tsing, translated by J. Takakusu. Munshiram Manoharlal, Delhi, India, 1966, p.162.

portance is the portion of the text designed to remove erroneous views produced from ignorance, for morality practised in ignorance does not result in liberation. However, through the combination of morality and wisdom (the understanding of emptiness) liberation is attained. This emptiness, the Ultimate Truth, is revealed through dispelling erroneous views.

Death, impermanence and opportune conditions form the subject matter for the subsequent verses of the text. Since life is transient like a bubble of water caught by the wind, Nāgārjuna exhorts the reader, who has obtained the opportune conditions which are prerequisites for the practice of Dharma, to strive for liberation without delay. If this human birth is not properly utilized, then one will continue to experience he sufferings of the six realms of Saṁsāra which are then described by Nāgārjuna. Such descriptions are commonly met with in texts of this kind. They are designed to produce a revulsion for worldly existence and a desire for liberation. The reader meeting with these descriptions for the first time should be warned against dismissing them as fanciful imagination, for they perform a vitally important function in the process of liberation. Since the highest goal of freedom and enlightenment cannot be achieved unless and until attachment to the world is relinquished, the detailed descriptions of the manifold sufferings experienced are necessary in order to produce that renunciation which is essential to tread the path to liberation. It should be remembered that the 'truth of suffering' is the first of the Four Noble Truths and the very cornerstone of the Buddhist religion.

Ācārya Nāgārjuna's letter concludes with a description of the path and the unequalled result to be gained through its practice. Morality, concentration and the wisdom arising from the understanding of the precious doctrine of Interdependent Origination comprise the path resulting in the exalted state of a Bodhisattva or Buddha.

Hence, as was said before, Ācārya Nāgārjuna's *Suhṛllekha* provides the aspirant who wishes to be acquainted with the essentials of the Buddhist path to liberation with a comprehensive summary of the principles of the Buddhist religion. The foundation of correct moral conduct and right understanding of the truth free from the obscurations of ignorance results in a transcendent mode of being in which not only is freedom from bondage and ignorance achieved, but also the capacity to nurture and mature all living beings that they may also attain enlightenment.

GENERAL OUTLINE OF NĀGĀRJUNA'S LETTER TO KING GAUTAMĪPUTRA

I. Encouragement to listen to the teaching

II. Direct Teaching

A. THE GENERAL PRACTICE OF VIRTUE

1. *Counsel to both monks and laymen*
   - a. Six things to remember
   - b. Counsel to remain steadfast in the ten precepts
   - c. Counsel to practise the six perfections of the Mahāyāna

2. *Counsel principally for laymen*
   - a. To have respect for one's parents
   - b. To observe continence on special days
   - c. To remove faults of mind
   - d. To practise heedfulness
   - e. To practise patience
   - f. To practise correct conduct of body, voice and mind
   - g. To know the qualities of one's associates
   - h. To abandon desire for the wives of others
     - (1) To control the sense-organs
       - (a) To perceive objects as impure rather than pure
       - (b) To protect the mind
       - (c) To consider faults of the object of attachment
     - (2) To uproot the causes of attachment
       - (a) Meditation to uproot the causes of attachment
       - (b) In praise of wisdom and morality
       - (c) To remain indifferent to the 'eight worldly *dharmas*'
       - (d) To acquire the wealth of the Holy Ones
       - (e) To give up behavior destructive of the wealth of the Holy Ones

(f) Remaining content is conducive to the wealth of the Holy Ones

i. To know the qualities of a prospective wife

3. *Counsel to both monks and laymen to practise the Dharma resulting in heaven and liberation*

a. The general practice of *Dharma*
   (1) To be watchful of the amount of food one takes
   (2) To strive without sleeping
   (3) To practise the limitless meditations
   (4) To practise the four concentrations
   (5) To reject or accept sins and virtues through viewing deeds as heavy or light
   (6) To abandon the five obscurations

b. To practise the *Dharma* resulting in liberation
   (1) To meditate on the five powers
   (2) To abandon pride which is an obstacle to attaining the five powers
   (3) To meditate in a way conducive to the right view
      (a) First, in brief
      (b) Second, the detailed explanation
         (1) To meditate on the four foundations of mindfulness
         (2) To meditate especially on the foundation of truth
         (3) To cast off the three fetters which are obstacles to liberation
         (4) To practise the three disciplines which are conducive to liberation
         (5) To protect mindfulness in regard to one's body

c. To make fruitful the foundation which has been achieved
   (1) To renounce attachment to one's body which is impermanent and without essence
   (2) To make fruitful the opportune conditions through realizing how rare they are
   (3) Counsel to the king to exert himself having achieved an extraordinarily good foundation

B. TO PRODUCE REVULSION FOR SAṂSĀRA

1. *First, in brief*
2. *Second, the detailed explanation*
   a. To consider the uncertainty in Saṃsāra
   b. To consider dissatisfaction
   c. To lose one's body again and again
   d. To be born again and again
   e. To consider ascent and descent through the various realms of Saṃsāra
   f. To consider one's solitary position
   g. To consider the sufferings experienced in the five realms
      (1) To consider the suffering in the hells
      (2) To consider the suffering of animals
      (3) To consider the suffering of hungry ghosts
      (4) To consider the suffering of gods
      (5) To consider the suffering of demigods
3, *To establish the understanding of Saṃsāra as unfortunate*

C. TO CONSIDER THE EXCELLENT QUALITIES OF NIRVĀṆA AND PRACTISE THE PATH RESULTING IN NIRVĀṆA

1. *General counsel with respect to all the disciplines which result in Nirvāṇa*
   a. To strive to attain Nirvāṇa
   b. Counsel to accumulate that which is needed to attain Nirvāṇa
      (1) To practise the seven branches of enlightenment
      (2) To indicate that Nirvāṇa is attained through the combination of quietude and insight
      (3) To reject speculation upon that which is inexpressible
      (4) To understand Interdependent Origination which frees one from Saṃsāra
      (5) To meditate on the Noble Eightfold Path
      (6) To consider the Four Noble Truths

(7) Not to hesitate to strive for Nirvāṇa
(8) Counsel in brief

2. *Counsel to practise the Path of the Mahāyāna*
   a. To enter the Mahāyāna Path through rejoicing in the demonstration of the Dharma
   b. To attain Nirvāṇa having gained Buddhahood and having accomplished the benefit of living beings

ĀCĀRYA NĀGĀRJUNA

Nāgārjuna's Letter To King Gautamīputra

With Explanatory Notes

I. Encouragement to Listen to the Teaching

O righteous and worthy one endowed with virtues, it is fitting you hear these few *Āryā* verses which I have composed so that you may aspire to the merit which rises from the *Sugata's* words. **1**

Ācārya Nāgārjuna opens his message to King Gautamīputra by urging him, as well as others, to pay careful attention to the teaching contained in this letter as it concerns the holy Dharma.

By the nature of the king's performance of virtuous deeds in previous lives, he has accumulated much merit which has now given him this opportunity to listen to Dharma (i.e., the Buddha's teaching). In the light of the king's temporal responsibilities, this short letter in *Āryā* verse has been written.

The aim of this teaching is to place the king and all other living beings on the path to liberation by means of the *Sugata's*[1] teaching. The Buddha's path is the proper method for attaining the higher realms[2] and liberation, because the merit and knowledge necessary for such attainments can only be accumulated by this path. Other schools rely only upon penance or meditation on *ātman* (self) in order to gain the higher realms and liberation, but these means produce an insufficient accumulation of merit and knowledge. These two accumulations can only be accomplished by the *Sugata's* way, because it is this path that fulfils the wishes of others.

1. *Sugata* is an epithet of the Buddha meaning one who has gone well to the further shore of the ocean of worldly existence.

2. The world of existence, Saṃsāra, consists of six realms subsumed under three spheres. i). *kāma-dhātu* : This is a sphere that includes the hells, the realm of hungry ghosts, the worlds of men and animals, and the six lower heavens. This is primarily a world of sensual desires. ii). *rūpa-dhātu* : This is a world of ethereal bodies which are obtained through the four concentrations (*dhyāna*). iii). *arūpa-dhātu* : This is a world of spiritual beings who are absorbed in transic states.

As is said by Mātṛceṭa in his *Śatapañcāśatka*,

> Your teaching, unlike others, is the only path pleasant in method, goodly in result, free from fault and fair in the beginning, middle and end.

* * *

For example, an image of the *Sugata*, if it be made of wood or whatever it be like, is worshipped by wise men. Likewise though this poem of mine lacks grace, do not despise it since it is based upon a discussion of the holy Dharma. 2

One should not disregard these words even though they may not be beautiful, because they embody a very important and holy teaching. Similarly, wise men worship any image of the *Sugata* whether it be made of gold, stone, wood or clay, whether it be beautiful or unattractive, or whether it be valuable or not.

However much of the Great Sage's words you may have listened to and may have even comprehended, still is not a white-painted (mansion) made whiter by the midnight moon ? 3

This letter should be studied even by the person who knows the precepts of the Great Sage so that his understanding of the teaching may be further clarified. This is especially true for one who, like the king, knows and practises Lord Buddha's teaching. Therefore, just as a white-painted mansion shines brighter by the light of the moon, likewise one's understanding of the teaching will become clearer.

II. Direct teaching

A. THE GENERAL PRACTICE OF VIRTUE

1. *Counsel to both monks and laymen*

a. Six things to remember

You should bring to mind the six things of remembrance : the Enlightened One, His Teaching, the Noble Assembly,

giving, morality, and gods; the heap of qualities of each of these six recollections was well-taught by the Conqueror. 4

One should take refuge in the Triple Gem daily as well as remembering these six just as they were taught in the scriptures.

As the Buddha is endowed with numerous qualities, various epithets are bestowed upon Him. Thus the Buddha is known as: *Jina* (Conqueror), *Bhagavān* (Blessed One), *Tathāgata* (One gone to 'suchness'), *Arhat* (Capable One), *Sugata* (Well-gone One), *Saṃyaksambuddha* (utmost, perfect Buddha), and *Atulya* (Matchless one). He is called *Jina*, because He has overcome all sin. He is called *Bhagavān*, because He has defeated the four *Māras*.[3] He is called *Tathāgata*, because whatever He said is true, since He is one with 'suchness' (*tathatā*). He is called *Arhat*, because He has vanquished the defilements of body, voice and mind. He is called *Sugata*, because He is one who has gone well to the further side of the ocean of Saṃsāra; who is the knower of Saṃsāra; who is the knower of Interdependent Origination; who is the knower of all things contained in Saṃsāra; and who sees Saṃsāra as a container and knows all the beings who are contained within it. He is called *Saṃyaksaṃbuddha*, because He is purely and perfectly enlightened. Furthermore, He is called *Atulya*, because He is compared to the driver of a horse-cart. Having first trained the horse to draw the cart, the driver then teaches the untamed horse to run straight and, then, to move in accordance with the driver's wishes. However, if it is impossible to place the horse in the harness, he leaves it alone for some time. The Buddha instructs living beings similarly. He first places on the Path those who should be on the path of religion, as well as causing lazy and unenergetic people to practise. Next, He corrects those who are proceeding on the wrong path, and places under control those who are uncontrollable. Lastly, the Buddha leaves alone those who want absolutely no help. In this way the *Sugata* is the 'matchless

3. *Māra* is that term which conveys the Buddhist conception of those internal and external factors which obstruct one's path to liberation. The four *Māras* are the defilements, the aggregates, death, and the deity (which in Buddhism may be likened to the devil).

driver' for training gods and men, who are His principal followers.

The two aspects of the Teaching (Dharma) are 'that which is shown by another' and 'that which is realized by oneself.' The former, the 'well-seen dharma', was shown by the Buddha. Therefore, one obtains wisdom by listening to, studying, contemplating and meditating on the Dharma that was taught by the Buddha. The latter, the 'well-received dharma', is attained by one's own realization. One who practises diligently will eventually gain Nirvāṇa, the 'well-received' result.

The Dharma path is naturally pure like intrinsically clear light. If one follows this path, he will see the truth rightly. This path is free from disease, because the defilements and their roots have been discarded. Having departed from these, one will attain a non-temporal state.

Dharma is divided into the two categories of teaching (i.e., the Truths of Suffering and of Origination) and of understanding (i.e., the Truths of Cessation and of the Path). The Truths of Cessation is realized by sages individually as it arises within them, therefore there is no definition of this Truth.

Those of the Noble Assembly (Saṅgha) possess these four special qualities: they keep a special moral code; they have well trained minds which remain fixed and unswerving; they possess great wisdom which enables them to see the truth; they have the same particular qualities, aims, ideas, philosophy, etc. These four qualities are natural to the Saṅgha. From this point of view people should worship monks as they are worthy of receiving alms. Furthermore, since they are possessed of trances and are an incomparable field for people to acquire merit, they are worthy of circumambulation and bowing to with joined palms.

The qualities of giving arise in the following ways: giving without miserliness, the giving itself, the effort one makes in giving, the gift itself, and the joy one has for the practice of giving.

The qualities of morality are that it is unimpaired, unmixed, faultless and unsullied. Sagacious people consider it praiseworthy, because, by upholding the moral discipline rightly, one's understanding of wisdom is increased and easy access to trances is produced.

The gods of the realms of desire (*kāma-dhātu*) and form (*rūpa-dhātu*) have much pleasure and many beautiful possessions. By having maintained moral discipline and attained trances in previous lives, they have gained such a high birth. Therefore, if one likens his own moral conduct and meditation to that of the gods, then one will remember their qualities in order to augment his own spiritual activity.

b. Counsel to remain steadfast in the ten precepts

Always practise the path of the ten virtuous deeds (performed) through body, voice and mind; refrain from alcohol, and also delight in a wholesome livehood. 5

It is necessary that one constantly practise the ten precepts. This is the practice of the right path which leads one to the right result. Therefore one must avoid these ten non-virtuous actions: three of body—killing, stealing, sexual misconduct; four of voice—lying, slander, malicious speech, idle speech; three of mind—covetousness, malevolence, erroneous views.

Knowing that wealth is unstable and devoid of essence, rightly bestow gifts upon monks, *brahmans*, the poor and friends; so for the next life there is no more excellent a kinsman than giving. 6

One should give to monks and *brahmans* because of their auspicious qualities; to parents, teachers and spiritual friends because of their kindness; and to hungry and sick people because of their need. As is said in the *Abhidharmakośa,*

> Immeasurable merit (will be obtained if one gives) to incarnate Bodhisattvas, or even to non-nobles (like) father, mother, sick people and Dharma teachers.

Furthermore, always keep in mind that wealth has no essence, because it is continually changing hands and is subject to decay and loss.

> **You should practise morality which is unimpaired, blameless, not mixed and unsullied—for morality is said to be the foundation of all virtues, just as the earth is (the support of both) animate and inanimate things.** 7

Just as one views the earth as the foundation of everything in the world, so one should view moral discipline as the foundation of all worldly and beyond-worldly qualities as well as trances and wisdom. As the *Śīlasaṃyuktasūtra* says,

> Just as a good vase is a receptacle of jewels, so moral discipline is the foundation of the growth of dharmas (i.e., virtues).

Furthermore, morality is the very basis for the final attainment of the freedom of Nirvāṇa.

Morality is endowed with four special qualities. First, it is called unimpaired because its rules are not broken and the faults which result in their transgression are avoided. Second, it is called blameless because attachment to the cause (i.e., the defilements) of breaking the vows is abandoned. Third, it is called not mixed because it is entirely free from non-virtuous thoughts. It is unmixed with the impure because the correctives of the defilements are constantly practised. Fourth, it is called unsullied because the attainment of supreme enlightenment rather than worldly wealth or activitiless Nirvāṇa[4] is aspired to.

c. Counsel to practise the six perfections of the Mahāyāna

Increase the measureless perfections of giving, morality, patience, energy, concentration, and wisdom, and thus

4. Activitiless Nirvāṇa is the *Śrāvaka's* Nirvāṇa — therefore personal freedom not complemented by the transcendental activities of a Buddha.

become the Lord of Conquerors who has reached the further shore of the ocean of existence. 8

All the paths of the Mahāyāna tradition are encompassed within the six perfections (*pāramitās*). These six are divided into two groups which are called the accumulation of merit (i.e., giving, morality and patience) and the accumulation of knowledge (i.e., concentration and wisdom). Energy is included in both groups as it is needed in all spheres of activities and qualities. Whether the Bodhisattvas, the great being, be in Saṃsāra or Nirvāṇa, all his requirements are fulfilled by these two accumulations.

While in Saṃsāra the Bodhisattva, who is possessed of the nature of the six perfections, avoids the faults of worldly existence in addition to helping other living beings. While remaining in Saṃsāra the Bodhisattva, by means of the perfections of giving, morality, patience and energy dwells in happiness. Having access to the Bliss-body (*Saṃbhogakāya*) and the Transformation-body (*Nirmāṇakāya*), he fulfils the needs of living beings. Having attained enlightenment the Bodhisattva dwells in happiness by means of the perfections of concentration and wisdom. Furthermore, having attained liberation the Bodhisattva will be able to acquire the Body of the Ultimate (*Dharmakāya*) through transcendental concentration and wisdom.

2. *Counsel principally for laymen*

a. To have respect for one's parents

The race of one who worships father and mother is in company of that of *Brahmā* and that of preceptors; through revering them one will win fame and later will attain the higher realms. 9

One should respect his parents, because they are the people who are the kindest to oneself in the present life. Those who give respect to their parents are gentle, blissful and will obtain many good qualities in this life and in the next. The Buddha declared that one who assists his parents is said to be of the *Brahmā*-race. As is said in the *Samādhirājasūtra*,

Always revere teachers, parents and likewise all sentient beings, (and) do not fall under the sway of pride (so that) the thirty-two auspicious marks of a Buddha may be obtained.

b. To observe continence on special days

Forsake killing, theft, sexual misconduct, lying, alcohol, attachment to food at improper times, enjoyment of high seats and beds, and all kinds of songs, dances and garlands. **10**

It is generally very difficult for the laymen to practise these eight precepts at all times. However, it is important that they be practised occasionally, and especially on religious holidays, such as the day commemorating the Buddha's attainment of enlightenment, etc. The significance of the practice of these eight precepts is shown in the following verse.

If you possess these eight features which resemble an *Arhat's* **morality, then, nourished by the religious vows, you will bestow on men and women the pleasant form of the gods of the realm of desire.** **11**

c. To remove faults of mind

Look upon these as enemies: miserliness, cunning, deceit, attachment to property, laziness, pride, sexual attachment, hatred, and arrogance of caste, form, learning, youth, and great power. **12**

One should look upon these thirteen faults as enemies:

(i) to be avaricious and miserly;

(ii) to hide one's own faults;

(iii) to show one's qualities by false methods;

(iv) to desire one's own body and health;

(v) to be lazy (i.e., to have no interest in the performance of virtuous actions);

(vi) to have pride (i.e., to pretend to have qualities which one does not possess);

(vii) to be lustful;

(viii) to be angry towards one's enemies;

(ix) to have pride of race;

(x) to have pride of form (i.e., to feel that one's body is better than that of another);

(xi) to have pride of learning;

(xii) to have pride of 'prime of life'; and

(xiii) to have pride of power.

d. To practise heedfulness

The Sage said that heedfulness is the source of the deathless and heedlessness is the source of death;[5] hence to increase your virtue, devotedly remain heedful. One who has formerly been heedless, but later becomes heedful—like Nanda, Aṅgulimāla, Ajātaśatru and Udayana—will also be resplendent like the moon free from clouds. 13-14

Even if one has performed non-virtuous deeds in the past, that should not prevent one from being heedful and mindful at the present time. For example, Nanda who had much desire, Aṅgulimāla who had much hatred, Ajātaśatru who killed his father, and Udayana who killed his mother, were, at first, all sinful people who were totally under the sway of their defilements.. However, they later entered the path of religion and became worthy men. Having committed so many sins in the past, people feel that they are now not worthy or capable of practising Dharma. However, through the examples of Nanda, Aṅgulimāla, Ajātaśatru and Udayana, this is shown not to be true.

e. To practise patience

Since there is no penance like patience, you must give anger no opportunity to arise. The Buddha said that by giving

5. Here 'source of death' means remaining in Saṃsāra.

up anger, one will attain the irreversible stage.[6] **15**

Burning one's body, diving into water, eating poor food such as roots and the like, and wearing poor cloths like garments of bark are not true acts of penance. It is said that such acts cannot even guarantee a higher rebirth in Saṃsāra. Rather, the greatest act of penance is patience. Therefore it is important to practise patience, especially when undesirable events—such as an attack on one's person, etc.—happens to oneself. In this way one will gain happiness, as shown in the following verse.

'I was abused by these (people), bound by them, defeated by them, they have snatched away my property'; thus harboring enmity produces quarrels, but one who gives up harboring enmity sleeps happily. **16**

As Śāntideva said in the *Bodhicaryāvatāra*,

> Whoever diligently destroys anger (will obtain) happiness in this and other lives.

f. To practise correct conduct of body, voice and mind

Recognize the mind to be like a drawing made on water, earth or stone; the first among these is excellent for those possessing the defilements, and the last for those desiring religion. **17**

The mind is of such a nature that various thoughts, remembrances, etc., can be categorized under three aspects which imply duration. That is, a mental event may be of very brief duration, of a relatively longer duration, or of an extensive duration. These three are exemplified by writing made on water which disappears as soon as the water is agitated, writing made on earth which disappears after a rainfall, etc., and writing

6. This is a stage which, once attained, signifies that the Bodhisattva can never again be bound by the defiled noose of worldly existence.

made on stone which endures for a very long time. Therefore it is said that one should always condition his defilements to occupy his mind just as writing remains on the surface of water. Furthermore, one should continually condition his mind to be occupied with virtuous deeds just as writing is engraved on the surface of a stone.

The Conqueror declared that pleasant, truthful and wrong are the three kinds of speech possessed by people—such words are like honey, flowers and filth. Abandon the last of these. 18

As sweet speech makes others happy, it is said to be pleasing like honey. As truthful speech is praiseworthy, it is said to be beautiful like a lovely flower. As wrong speech is unwholesome it is declared to be repulsive like excrement. One should adhere to sweet and truthful speech, but abandon wrong speech.

Four categories of persons are seen (who move) from: light to extreme light, dark to extreme dark, light to extreme dark and dark to extreme light; be the first among these. 19

(i) The person as categorized as moving from light to extreme light: Having performed virtuous actions in the past, this person has now obtained a fortunate birth. Further, in the present life he continues to perform virtuous activities and remains steadfast in the Dharma path. As a result of this, he will not only gain a higher rebirth but also eventually liberation. Finally, this person will achieve the ultimate attainment of Buddhahood.

(ii) The person as categorized as moving from dark to extreme dark: Having been born in one of the states of woe, this unfortunate person continues to practise non-virtuous actions. This will result in lower rebirths and still fewer advantageous conditions.

(iii) The person as categorized as moving from light to extreme dark: Having performed virtuous actions in the past, this person has now obtained a fortunate birth. However, in the present life he performs non-virtuous actions which will result in rebirth into the lower realms.

(iv) The person as categorized as moving from dark to extreme light: This person, born in less fortunate circumstances with few opportunities to practise Dharma, tries to keep the precepts and do virtuous actions in the present life. As a result of this, he will gain rebirth into a higher realm.

g. To know the qualities of one's associates

Persons should be understood to be like mango fruits which are: unripened yet seemingly ripe, ripened yet seemingly unripe, unripened and appearing to be unripe, and ripened ones which also appear to be ripe. 20

Always examine the nature of other people before taking them as friends. As exemplified by the mango fruit, persons correspondingly are:

(i) the intentions of the person are not good, but their actions are good;

(ii) the intentions of the person are good, but their actions are not good;

(iii) neither the intentions nor the actions of the person are good;

(iv) both the intentions and the actions of the person are good.

One should be like the fourth and should have friends with the same qualities.

h. To abandon desire for the wives of others

(1) To control the sense-organs

(a) To perceive objects as impure rather than pure

Do not look upon another's wife; however, should you see her, think of her according to her age—thus as mother, daughter or sister. If lust persists, then meditate well on impurity. 21

In order to control one's own defilements, it is necessary to be watchful of oneself. For example, one should not look upon another's wife covetously. However, if the sight of such a woman creates a desire within oneself, then by bringing to mind the faults of the desires of this life (as well as their result in the next life), one is able to overcome the defilement of desire. If this does not subdue the desire, one should then regard the woman according to her age as either mother, daughter or sister. If one still cannot control the desire, then one must consider the woman as unwholesome in the sense of being only a pile of flesh, bones, blood, etc., and that she is impermanent. Further, one should consider that she will become ugly, old and will eventually die. Having died she will become a skeleton, and at that time not only will one not want to see her but the sight of her will inspire fear. Reflecting thus, one will subdue the defilement of desire.

(b) To protect the mind

Protect the unsteady mind just as (you would protect) learning, a son, a treasure, or life; withdraw the mind from sensual pleasures just as (you would withdraw yourself) from a vicious (snake), poison, a weapon, an enemy or fire. 22

It is of utmost importance to guard one's own mind. Having considered one's mind as his only wealth, as one's own beloved children, as a great treasure of jewels, or even as life itself, one should protect his mind so as not to become entangled in the defilements of actions, speech and thought.

The Lord of Conquerors declared desires to be like the *Kimbu* fruits, for they are the cause of misery; since these iron chains bind worldlings in the prison of Saṃsāra, renounce them. 23

Having experienced a pleasure or that which at first seemed to be pleasurable, one learns that this inevitably create only trouble. Lord Buddha said, "The *Kimbu* fruit is like worldly pleasure. The skin of the *Kimbu* fruit is very beautiful and good, but the inside is poisonous and leads to disaster. Therefore, one should give up worldly pleasure". If one continues to grasp for pleasures, one will be securely bound by the iron chains of saṃsāra and will never be free. As Śāntideva said in the *Bodhicaryāvatāra*,

> Desires will produce evil consequences in this life and in the next also: in this life (one will be) killed, bound and cut, and in the next (one) will obtain the hells, etc.

* * *

(In choosing) between the one who conquers (attachment to) the ever unsteady and momentary objects of the six sense-organs and the one who conquers the enemy's army in battle, the wise know the first to be a far greater hero. 24

One must not allow his senses to become entangled with the defilements. If one combats his defilements by disengaging his senses from them, the battle has then been won. If one can act in such a manner, he is braver and more heroic than the victor on the battlefield. Even animals can win in battle, but few are able to conquer the senses.

(c) To consider the faults of the object of attachment and of the subject who is attached

Look upon the body of a young maiden apart from ornaments (and clothing) to be like a totally impure vessel covered with skin, difficult to satisfy, bad smelling, and with impurities issuing from the nine (bodily) doors. 25

The remedy for the desire for women should be considered in the following manner. First, one should imagine a woman with beautiful clothes and ornaments, but reflect that inside she is impure. Secondly, having taken away the decorations, one discovers that she is impure without as well as within. In other words, she is only a heap of flesh, bones, blood, etc. A woman is truly similar to a beautiful vase that is filled with impurities.

Know that just as the insect-ridden leper wholly depends on fire for the sake of happiness, similarly clinging to desires will bring no peace. 26

The more one enjoys worldly pleasures, the more he wants them. This is like a thirsty man who drinks salt water which only increases his thirst. In this way, worldly pleasures are never satisfactory. As is said in the *'khor.lo.sgyur.ba'i. gtam.zhes.pa'i. mdo.*,

> Sentient beings who rely upon passion will further increase their desires; if one closely clings to the object (of desire) his desire will never be satisfied.

One should try to free his mind from desires for worldly pleasures by first thinking of the bad results which they will bring. Having considered desire in this way, then try to put a stop to that desire immediately. Worldly pleasures lead only to more suffering, as the placing of a leprous arm in a fire.

(2) To uproot the causes of attachment

(a) Meditation to uproot the causes of attachment

Be skilled in rightly perceiving things with the understanding of the Ultimate (Truth), for there is no other practice possessing comparable quality. 27

One should look for the truth of all *dharmas*[7] (i.e., the five aggregates[8] and external things). If one carefully examines all

7. The term *dharma*, which in Buddhism has various meanings, may be understood to mean here the constituent elements of existence.

8. The five constituents (i.e.. aggregates, Tib. phung. po., Skt. skandha) which comprise the empirical individual are :

(1) form, Tib. gzugs., Skt. rūpa;
(2) feelings, Tib. tshor. ba., Skt. vedanā;
(3) perception, Tib. 'du. shes., Skt. saṁjñā;
(4) predispositions, Tib. 'du. byed., Skt. saṁskāra;
(5) consciousness, Tib. rnam. par. shes. pa., Skt. vijñāna.

dharmas, then he will see that not a single atom really exists. If one views dharmas with the understanding of the Ultimate Truth and meditates on emptiness (*Śūnyatā*), then there is no better teaching to purify *karma* and to destroy the defilements. Without a doubt, the best teaching (*dharma*) is the understanding of emptiness. As is said in the *Mūla-madhyamaka-kārikā*,

> *Karma* and defilements (arise) from conceptualizations, these (arise) from mental creations, and creations are extinguished by emptiness.

Though everything in Saṃsāra is ultimately not existent, nevertheless things as they appear and are experienced (i.e., things arisen from causes and conditions) are not denied. When seen as Interdependent Origination everything is dependent on other things for its existence (that is, everything is devoid of own-being). The essence of Lord Buddha's teaching is in the 'twelve links of Interdependent Origination'. The reason for this is: (i). Things are not born from themselves (i.e., the cause and the effect are not identical); (ii) Things are not born from others (i.e., the cause and the effect are not different); (iii) Things are not born both from themselves and from others (i.e., the cause and the effect are not both identical and different); and (iv) Things are not born neither from themselves nor from others (i.e., the cause and the effect being neither identical nor different — therefore, arising without cause).

According to the Mādhyamika, these doctrines are proven false since no truth is found in them. In fact, the Mādhyamika has no doctrine concerning the Ultimate Truth of its own to prove, but only examines those of others.

The Ultimate Truth is impossible to explain through logic, reason, words, example, etc. No one can tell another what the Ultimate Truth is. It can only be seen through one's own realization which is termed the 'self-seen wisdom'.

(b) In praise of wisdom and morality

The person possessing high caste, beautiful form and learning is not respected if he lacks wisdom and morality; however,

one who possesses these two qualities, even though lacking the other qualities, is worshipped. **28**

Sakya Pandita Kunga Gyaltsen Pal Zangpo said in the *legs. bshad.rin. po.che'i.gter.*,

> Even though one possess high caste, lineage, family, good form, and youth, if one does not have knowledge he is not handsome.

One is not thought to be a superior person, nor considered worthy of worship, if he is born in a high family or possesses a good complexion, much wealth, much learning, many virtues, fame, etc. However, those who understand *śūnyatā*, though they may not possess the above qualities are worthy of worship. As is said in *Jātaka*,

> If one does not practise well giving, moral discipline, etc., even though (he possess) high lineage, good form, qualities of youth, very great strength, and wealth still he will never obtain happiness in his next life. Even though one possess low lineage, etc., if one is not attached to sin and possesses well the qualities of giving, moral discipline, etc., then just as the rivers fill the ocean during the monsoon season so he will certainly increase his happiness in the next life.

Wisdom and morality have been praised by Ācārya Nāgārjuna for those who wish to understand the Ultimate Truth. One cannot be holy if he lacks wisdom and morality. Since wisdom reveals that which is to be accepted and that which to be abandoned, it is essential for the attainment of sainthood.

(c) To remain indifferent to the 'eight worldly *dharmas*'

O knower of the world, the eight worldly ***dharmas*****—gain, loss, happiness, unhappiness, sweet words, harsh words,**

praise, and blame—should be regarded equally as (they) are not worthy of your mind. **29**

Of the 'eight worldly *dharmas*', the four which are desired by worldlings are:

(i) gain (i.e., acquisition of material wealth, etc.);
(ii) pleasure or happiness;
(iii) sweet or pleasing speech (i.e., fame, etc.);
(iv) praise.

If one receives any of these four, he becomes happy. One always strives and seeks for these, and if he obtains them, he is very pleased. However, of the 'eight worldly *dharmas*', the four which are not desired are:

(i) loss of wealth, etc.;
(ii) unhappiness or pain (i.e., misery of both mind and body);
(iii) harsh or unpleasant speech (i.e., slander, notoriety, contempt, etc.);
(iv) blame or criticism.

These four are always feared and result in great unhappiness when they are experienced. However this is not a suitable attitude for one who wishes to practise religion. As Śāntideva said in the *Bodhicaryāvatāra*,

> Even though one acquire many gains, fame and praise, it is uncertain where the accumulation of fame and wealth will be lost.

One should neither hope for the first four conditions, nor fear the last four. Finding no difference among them — neither striving for the four pleasant ones nor avoiding the four unpleasant ones — the person practising religion should regard the 'eight worldly *dharmas*' as equal.

Do not commit sins for the sake of *brahmans*, monks, gods, guests, parents, sons, queen, or attendants, because there is not anyone to share the result of hell. **30**

One should avoid collecting sins for one's own ends or for the sake of others, whether they be preceptors, monks, teachers, deities, mother, father, queen, etc. Even if one were to commit a sin for another, the result of that action is still borne by one-self and not by other. One must bear the full result of any sins himself, just as one must bear the suffering of illness alone. As it is said in *Sūtra*,

> (The result of) deeds will not be ripened upon earth, water or stone, but only upon (one's) own aggregates.

It may be asked, "If sins produce disastrous results, why are they not produced immediately"? It is replied, "There are three types of results which ripen from non-virtuous actions. First, there are some deeds the results of which will appear in this very lifetime. For instance, if one were to commit a sinful deed early in his life, the result could appear towards the end of his life. Second, there are some deeds performed in this life the results of which will appear in the subsequent life. Lastly, there are some deeds performed in this life the results of which will appear only after several lifetimes."

Though some sinful deeds performed will not wound you immediately like a weapon, still any result (arising) from those sinful actions will become manifest when the time of death befalls. 31

Though one will not experience immediate retribution for sinful deeds committed, still — when one is caught by the Lord of Death at the time of one's demise — one will experience their disastrous results, such as the intense suffering of the hells. At that time, one will surely know the results of his sins. Some people think that since the results of sinful actions are not perceived, they will not experience them. However, this is not so!

(d) To acquire the wealth of the Holy Ones

The Sage said that faith, morality, giving, study, modesty, humility, and wisdom are the seven unblemished properties; recognize other common properties to be meaningless. 32

The seven Noble Wealths are:

(i) belief in the Triple Gem (i.e., Buddha, Dharma and Saṅgha) the law of *Karma* and the phenomenal and ultimate truths;

(ii) adherence to the moral code;

(iii) bestowing gifts, alms, etc.;

(iv) the study of *Dharma*;

(v) avoidance of non-virtuous actions out of one's own sense of aversion and shame;

(vi) avoidance of non-virtuous actions for fear of being condemned by others;

(vii) the ability to discriminate between virtuous and non-virtuous deeds so as to determine the right course of action.

These practices, performed without selfish aims and intentions, are very beneficial. Though one may not be rich in gold and silver, still if one has these seven he possesses the most excellent among all treasures. Furthermore, the seven wealths are conditions which are conducive to attaining the great bliss of Nirvāṇa which is without suffering.

(e) To give up behavior destructive of the wealth of the Holy Ones

Abandon these six which result in loss of fame and birth in evil states: gambling participation in festivals, laziness, association with sinful friends, alcohol, and walking in the night. 33

The six things which can destroy the 'seven noble wealths' are:

(i) gambling,

(ii) attendance of fairs and festivals,

(iii) laziness,

(iv) association with sinful friends who contribute to one's defilements,

(v) drinking alcohol, and

(vi) roaming around in the night without any purpose.

These six faults will be a cause for one to lose fame, etc., in this life, as well as being a cause for one's rebirth into lower realms in his subsequent life. Therefore one should avoid these six.

(f) Remaining content is conducive to the wealth of the Holy Ones

The Preceptor of gods and men said that satisfaction is the most excellent among all riches, so always be satisfied; if content through possessing no wealth, one is truly rich. 34

One should always be satisfied with whatever one possesses. Greed will always cause one to feel dissatisfied and unhappy. Moreover, anxiety will arise from the desire to acquire more wealth, protect it, etc. Even though a person be poor, if he is content with what he has, then he possesses the greatest wealth and is happy. As is said in the *Bodhicaryāvatāra*,

> It should be known that wealth is full of evil consequences through the sufferings of gathering, guarding and losing it; having become agitated by the desire for wealth, (one) will not have the opportunity to be free from the sufferings of existence.

* * *

O gracious king, just as the most excellent of *Nāgas* suffers in accordance with the number of heads he has acquired, just so one suffers in accordance with the number of properties acquired; however, it is not so for one with few desires. 35

One will suffer in proportion to the amount of superfluous property he acquires. This is exemplified by the *Nāga*[9] kings who suffer in accordance with the number of heads they possess. Therefore, one should be watchful of his desires.

9. According to Indian thought *Nāgas* are creatures which possess bodies that are half human and half snake. They are believed to dwell in the earth and to influence rainfall, protect wealth, etc.

i. To know the qualities of a prospective wife

Avoid these three kinds of wives: one who, like an executioner, is naturally associated with the enemy; one who, like a queen, disrespects the husband; and one who, like a thief, steals even small things. (The type of wife) to revere as a family deity is the one who is kind like a sister, one who is dear like a friend, one who wishes your benefit like a mother, or one who is subject to you like a servant. 36-37

As this letter is written for laymen, this counsel is given. The three kinds of women that one should not take as wives are:

(i) one who is naturally linked with enemies who desire the demise of the husband;

(ii) one who always wishes to govern and to be thought of as the foremost, thereby disrespecting the husband;

(iii) one who steals even small things like a thief.

3. *Counsel to both monks and laymen to practise the Dharma resulting in heaven and liberation*

a. The general practice of *Dharma*

(1) To be watchful of the amount of food one takes

Understanding food to be like medicine, neither use it with hatred, nor attachment, nor for might, pride or beauty, but solely for maintaining the body. 38

Keeping in mind that food is only medicine for the illness of hunger, one should always eat moderately. One should neither eat with the intention of acquiring beauty, physical strength or pride nor with any thought of desire or hatred. Therefore one should eat for the purpose of sustaining the body so as to practise *Dharma*. As Śāntideva said in the *Bodhicaryāvatāra*,

> Share (food) with those fallen into evil states, those without protection and with fellow ascetics; eat moderately and give (everything) except three robes.

(2) To strive without sleeping

O righteous one, after (usefully) spending the whole day and the beginning and end of the night, mindfully sleep only in the middle (period), so even the time of sleep will not be fruitless. 39

Having a great revulsion for Saṃsāra, one should constantly strive for enlightenment. Through neither wasting day nor night, one should use all of one's time for practising the path leading to liberation. Furthermore, one should sleep in the middle part of the night with the thought of not sleeping too long and of using that sleep as a part of his path to liberation.

As is said in the *Bodhicaryāvatāra*,

> Sleep as the Protector slept (at the time of His) Nirvāṇa in whatever direction desired; before sleeping conscientiously and firmly impress on the mind to arise early.

(3) To practise the limitless meditations

Always meditate rightly on love, compassion, joy, and equanimity; even if the supreme (state) is not gained in this way, still the happiness of the world of *Brahmā* will be attained. 40

Limitless meditation includes the following four parts.

(i) Love : The wish for all sentient beings to be happy and have the cause of happiness.

(ii) Compassion : The wish for all sentient beings to depart from suffering and the cause of suffering.

(iii) Joy : The wish for all sentient beings to feel joyous, because they possess the cause of happiness.

(iv) Equanimity : One regards all sentient beings with complete equanimity. That is, one leaves attachment for dear ones and hatred for enemies and treats all equally.

This meditation is called limitless because its object, sentient beings, is limitless. Moreover, it is called limitless because, through meditating in this way, one receives incalculable merit.

Through this practice one will eventually attain enlightenment. Even if enlightenment is not achieved quickly, one will gain the four stations of *Brahmā*. In other words, one will attain rebirth in the *rūpa-dhātu* which is free from the sufferings experienced in the *kāma-dhātu*.

(4) To practise the four concentrations

Having given up the pleasures, joys and sufferings of the realm of desire by means of the four concentrations, the fortunate levels of the gods—*Brahmā*, *Ābhāsvara*, *Śubhakṛtsna* and *Bṛhatphala*—will be obtained. **41**

Through the correctives of consideration and investigation, one abandons the desire and violence of the realm of desire. One who attains the first concentration (*dhyāna*) born from the trance (*samādhi*) of one-pointedness of mind possesses investigation, pleasure and joy. At this stage one has abandoned consideration. Through the corrective of inner purification, one abandons investigation. Then one who attains the second concentration born from the trance of one-pointedness of mind possesses pleasure and joy. Through the correctives of indifference, mindfulness and remembrance, one abandons pleasure. Having attained the third concentration born from the trance of one-pointedness of mind, one possesses joy. Through the correctives of remembrance and indifference to feelings, one abandons joy and suffering. Having attained the fourth concentration born from the trance of one-pointedness of mind, one possesses indifference to feelings.

(5) To reject or accept sins and virtues through viewing deeds as heavy or light

From the foundation of these five great factors—persistence, intention, unopposed, endowed with qualities, and

beneficiaries—virtuous and non-virtuous deeds arise (in great measure); therefore, strive to do virtuous actions. 42

The five modifying factors are as follows :

(i) One should perform virtuous actions all of the time.

(ii) One should have great intention to do virtuous actions and little intention to do non-virtuous actions.

(iii) Without contradiction, one should always do virtuous actions.

(iv) One should do virtuous actions for that which is éndowed with excellent qualities, like the Triple Gem, etc.

(v) One should do more for his benefactors, such as parents and religious persons, etc., because greater merit is accumulated through performing good deeds for them. However, if one harms his parents of religious persons, then greater sin is accumulated. Further, actions done modified by any of these five are the foundation of the accumulation of virtue and non-virtue in great proportion.

Understand that a small measure of salt changes the taste of a little water while not that of the Ganges River; similarly, a small sinful deed (will not spoil) a vast root of virtue. 43

One should avoid non-virtuous actions and do great virtuous ones. For example, a small quantity of salt in a small amount of water gives the water a salty taste, but that quantity of salt cannot change the taste of a huge river. In this same manner, small deeds of sin are impossible to hide by a small amount of virtue, while those deeds of sin are made invisible by great virtuous actions.

(6) To abandon the five obscurations

Be aware that these five obscurations are thieves which steal the wealth of virtue : insolence and regret, harmful thoughts, apathy and sleepiness, attachment, and doubt. 44

The five obscurations are :

(i) Preoccupied with worldly pleasures, one destroys his virtues through insolence and regretting virtuous deeds which were done in the past.

(ii) One wishes ill towards his enemies.

(iii) Having heaviness of body and mind, one takes no interest in doing virtuous works. Also, one sleeps too much.

(iv) One has attachment to material things and is lustful.

(v) One has doubt about the Truth.

These five are obscurations to one's path. As it is disastrous to lose one's wealth of virtue, one should avoid these obscurations which are like thieves.

b. To practise the Dharma resulting in liberation

(1) To meditate on the five powers

Assiduously perform the five most excellent practices—faith, energy, mindfulness, trance, and wisdom. These are called strength, power, and also the attained summit. 45

The five powers leading to spiritual progress are:

(i) One believes in the Truth with great faith.

(ii) In order to realize the Truth, one must expend much effort and enthusiasm.

(iii) One should not forget what he has experienced of the Truth.

(iv) One must produce one-pointed concentration upon that experience.

(v) One must discern through wisdom the reality of the Truth which one has experienced.

The four different levels through which one progresses are called :

(i) heat (Tib. drod., Skt. ūsmā),

(ii) top (Tib. rtse. mo., Skt. mūrdha),

(iii) patience (Tib. bzod. pa., Skt. kṣānti),

(iv) most excellent (Tib. chos. mchog., Skt. agradharma).

(i) Since one is able to see more of the truth when practising at level of 'heat', the practice is likened to the sense-organs. This level is like the heat that foreshadows the burning away of the defilements. For example, when rubbing two sticks together, heat is produced before the actual fire begins.

(ii) One's root of virtue is increased by means of this knowledge when practising at the level known as 'top'. At this level the defilements and the fire of knowledge are in equilibrium.

(iii) One overcomes the many obstacles by using these five as powers when practising at the level of 'patience'. At this level the fire of knowledge has become stronger than the defilements and burns them away.

(iv) One has obtained the real cause of the Noble Path when practising at the level of 'most excellent'. At this level the defilements are completely destroyed. This is the most excellent among worldly achievements.

Having accomplished these four levels, one has become a Holy One and has thus attained the first *bhūmi*.[10]

(2) To abandon pride which is an obstacle to attaining the five powers.

> **"Thus actions done by oneself (are the cause) of not passing beyond disease, old age, death and separation from the dear." Arrogance will not arise by means of the corrective of this repeated thought. 46**

One should create the corrective for destroying the defilements and, so, free oneself from them. In order to do this, examination and meditation are necessary. For instance, one must think that one is never free of disease, old age and death, and suffering. Also, one should think that any virtuous or non-virtuous action performed will affect him alone and will be shared by no one else. One should think in this way again and again, and so create the corrective for his defilements.

10. There are ten stages, *bhūmi*, through which a Bodhisattva progresses on his way to Buddhahood. At the time of obtaining the first stage, the Bodhisattva is called a Holy One (*ārya*).

(3) To meditate in a way conducive to the right view

(a) First, in brief

Follow the right view if heaven and liberation are desired, for even persons doing meritorious deeds through the wrong view will have all terrible results. 47

If one desires a higher birth in his next life, or wishes for final liberation, then one must practise the root of all the 'white *dharmas*' (virtues). In other words, one must observe the law of *Karma* which is the 'right worldly view'. Also, one must understand the nature of all *dharmas* to be emptiness which is the 'ultimate right view'. So if one does not accept the law of *Karma* and *Śūnyatā* (emptiness), then he will have terrible results, even though he has accumulated much merit.

(b) Second, the detailed explanation

(1) To meditate on the four foundations of mindfulness

Know that in reality human beings are unhappy, impermanent, devoid of self, and impure; those who forsake mindfulness are ruined through wrongly viewing these four. 48

If one thinks carefully he will see that human beings are never happy and are always suffering. He will observe the following four.

(i) One is suffering.

(ii) One is impermanent.

(iii) One has no self as all living beings are devoid of a self.

(iv) One is impure (i.e., being only a pile of flesh, blood, bones, etc.).

If one thinks in the following manner, then he holds the four wrong views.

(i) One is happy.

(ii) One is permanent.

(iii) One has a self.

(iv) One is clean.

If one always maintains these four wrong views, then he will never be free from the suffering and evil consequences of Saṃsāra. As Śāntideva said in the *Bodhicaryāvatāra*,

> So never allow mindfulness to depart from the door of the mind. If it departs, recollect and earnestly meditate upon the miseries of the states of woe.

(2) To meditate especially on the foundation of Ṭruth

Thus it has been said: "The form is not the self, the self does not possess the form, the self does not dwell in the form, and the form does not dwell in the self", in this manner also understand the four remaining aggregates as empty. 49

In a *Sūtra* it says, "The form is not 'I', etc.". This means:

(i) The form is not the self (i.e., I, ego, soul, etc.). If the form dies, then the self would also die. For this reason, the form cannot be the self. Again, there would be many I's if the form were the I.

(ii) The form is not possessed by the self. The form and the self have no connection. The self does not own the form, because the form acts of its own accord or by other factors. Also, it cannot be said that the self is different from the form because the self is never seen apart from it.

(iii) The self does not abide in the form. One should examine the aggregates and the self in order to see if they are identical or different.

(iv) The form does not abide in the self. This would be possible only if one were able to prove that the self and the aggregates are different.

By means of these four methods, one is able to see that form, which is produced and destroyed, is devoid of a self. Furthermore, the four remaining aggregates (i.e., feeling, perception, predispositions, and consciousness) should be examined in a similar way.

Know that the aggregates originated neither from chance, time, Nature, intrinsic character, God, nor without cause, but from ignorant deeds and craving. 50

The aggregates, such as form and the like, did not originate by accidentally falling from the sky, did not originate from eternal time, did not originate from a permanent nature, did not originate from intrinsic character, and did not originate from an ever-existing God. If one accepts that the aggregates arose from these causes, it will be faulty as they will have arisen from contradictory causes. Furthermore, the aggregates are not originated without a cause since, if this were so, they would always exist or not exist.

Again, the aggregates did not originate from time since they have their own causes and conditions. Apart from these, time cannot be spoken of. Further, in refutation of the *Sāṃkhya* philosophy, if Nature (*prakṛti*) were the producer of things it would not be eternal.

The accumulation of actions through ignorance is the cause of the aggregates. This ignorance is the moisture which enables the seed of craving to grow, so causing one to be born again and again.

(3) To cast off the three fetters which are obstacles to liberation

Understand these three to be fetters (to Saṃsāra) and obstacles to the gates of the city of liberation: adhering solely to morality and asceticism, mistaken view of self-individuality and doubt. **51**

If one adheres to these three, they will be the greatest obstacles to attaining liberation. For example, if one has somewhere to go, it will be impossible to reach the desired destination if the following three are present:

(i) One does not want to go.

(ii) One is following a wrong path.

(iii) One has doubts about the path that he is following. Due to these obstacles, one will never arrive at his destination.

With regard to religion these three, which will interfere with one's gaining liberation, are explained thus:

(i) One believes that following certain rules, adhering to

moral discipline, doing penance, or performing physical austerities will be sufficient for gaining the path to liberation. However, this person does not practise meditation, accumulate merit and wisdom, and the like, which are necessary for the path.

(ii) One continues to think of his five aggregates as real, thus leading one to conceive of an 'I' and a 'my'. With thoughts like these, one treads the wrong path and holds the wrong view.

(iii) One is doubtful about the path he is following.

If these three great obstacles remain, then the door to liberation is closed.

(4) To practise the three disciplines which are conducive to liberation

Since liberation depends on oneself and not on any help from others, cultivate the fourfold truth through possessing study, morality and concentration. 52

The path to liberation is mainly dependent on oneself. In order to attain this path one must free his own mind from the defilements. For this purpose, one must be familiar with the methods of the path.

No one can help another, or take another by the hand, in order to put one on the path to liberation. One must do everything by himself. What should one do to attain this path ? First, one must have the foundation of right moral conduct. Beyond that, one has to study the *sūtras*, and scriptures of qualified authorities. By studying, understanding and, especially, meditating on these texts, then the path to liberation will arise. Further, one is able to attain liberation if he meditates on the Four Noble Truths which have four characteristics each,[11] and, especially, on the Ultimate Truth which is *Śūnyatā*.

11. The four characteristics of the Truth of Suffering are:

(1) impermanence: The five aggregates are impermanent, because they are born at a particular time.

(2) suffering: The five aggregates are full of suffering, because they are subject to deeds and defilements.

(3) empty: The five aggregates are empty, because they are devoid of a self. (contd.)

One should realize and practise the path rightly according to the Four Noble Truths, thus:

(i) one has to understand suffering;

(ii) one has to renounce the cause of suffering which is craving;

(iii) one has to discover and follow the Truth;

(iv) one has to tread the path to liberation.

Always be disciplined in the highest morality, highest wisdom and highest trance; more than one hundred and fifty disciplines[12] are verily included within these three. 53

(4) devoid of self: There is no self in its own-being.

The four characteristics of the Truth of Origination are:

(1) causation: Craving is the cause of origination, because it is the root of suffering.

(2) origination: Craving is the origin of all suffering, because it produces sufferings again and again.

(3) production: Craving is the producer, because it produces intense suffering.

(4) becoming: The craving for becoming is a condition supporting the cause.

The four characteristics of the Truth of Cessation are:

(1) cessation: Cessation is freedom from sufferings which have been removed by the correctives.

(2) quietude: Cessation is freedom from afflictions, since the defilements have been removed.

(3) excellent: Cessation is excellent, because it is liberation which is of the nature of joy and happiness.

(4) deliverance: Cessation is release, because it is liberated from the defilements, etc., which have been finally removed.

The four characteristics of the Truth of the Path are:

(1) path: Wisdom is the direct realization of selflessness which places one on the path leading to the city of liberation.

(2) correct method: Wisdom is the direct corrective for the defilements.

(3) accomplishment: Wisdom is accomplishment, because it rightly accomplishes the purification of the mind.

(4) release: Wisdom removes suffering, as it certainly releases one from the triple world.

12. The commentary indicates that this refers to the root disciplines of a monk as mentioned in the *Vinaya*.

One should study the three subjects.

(i) The subject of *Vinaya* is moral conduct. There are different codes for different people, viz., laymen, novices and monks.

(ii) The subject of *Abhidharma* is the wisdom which discerns that all things are devoid of a self. One must try to understand that, in reality, everything is devoid of self, i.e., the absence of a self in 'persons' as well as in 'things' (*dharmas*).

(iii) The subject of *sūtras* is meditation, and how one is to focus the mind. This is the path to attain the four *dhyānas* (i.e., states of concentration).

All the necessary methods for acquiring the path to liberation are included in these three.

(5) To protect mindfulness in regard to one's body

O lord, mindfulness regarding the body was taught to be the only path (to liberation) by the *Sugata*. Since the loss of mindfulness will destroy all virtues, guard it well through steadfastness. 54

Mindfulness should be maintained when performing any bodily action. All the *Sugatas* have said that it is very important to remember what one should do. Therefore, one should earnestly be mindful of which actions are to be performed, which are to be abandoned, etc. If one remains mindful, all virtues will surely follow. As is said in the *Bodhicaryāvatāra*,

> Having tightly bound the elephant of mind by the rope of thorough mindfulness, all fears will become non-existent and all virtues will come into (one's) hands.

c. To make fruitful the foundation which has been achieved

(1) To renounce attachment to one's body which is impermanent and without essence

Life is impermanent since (it is beset by) many misfortunes like a bubble of water caught by the wind; that one inhales after exhaling and awakens from sleep is wonderful. 55

One must think about impermanence and death in order to cultivate the aforementioned mindfulness. It is not suitable to have attachment for one's life and body, because life is impermanent and the body has no essence. Life is extremely transient, because there are many external factors which can cause death, such as attack from enemies, accidents, contact with poisons, etc. With this in mind, it is apparent that there are many causes which can result in death. As is said in the *Ratnāvalī*,

> To live with *Yama* (who is) the cause (of death) is like a lamp existing with a violent wind.

Though one may have no intention of harming oneself, he may eat a poisonous fruit which he thought would nourish him, but which, in fact, only harms him. Furthermore, there are many internal conditions which can cause death, such as: bile, phlegm, cold, fever, etc.

Life is like a bubble of water caught by the wind which can disappear at any moment. One should be very grateful that when he exhales, he does not die before inhaling again. Further one should think it a wonderful event that when one goes to sleep at night, he does not die before waking up in the morning.

> **Know that the insubstantial body at the end—becoming ashes, dried, putrid or impure—will be completely destroyed and despoiled (and) its constituents dispersed. 56**

One day one's body will be burned, buried, dried, eaten, or dismembered. As Candrakīrti said in the *Bodhisattva-yogacaryā-catuḥśataka-ṭīkā*,

> Having been conceived, from the first night a hero of men dwells in the worldly womb, he ceaselessly approaches his death day by day.

In view of this, there is no reason for attachment to this particular body. This body will not always be with one, for it is definitely not an eternal thing. Thus the body has no essence, and attachment to it is not proper. As is said in the *Bodhicaryāvatāra*,

> Your excrement is unsuitable to eat, your blood also is unsuitable to drink, further, your entrails are unsuitable to suck, so of what use is your body!

* * *

Since not even ash will remain as all things—the earth, *Mount Sumeru* and the oceans—will be consumed by the flames of the seven suns,[13] what need to say anything of very frail men. 57

Very large and solid substances like the earth and the mountains, or even the oceans, arise and perish. Thus everything is impermanent. Therefore one's soft, fragile body will certainly be destroyed.

O best of men, since everything is impermanent, devoid of self, refugeless, protectorless, and homeless, free your mind from Saṃsāra which is like the pithless plantain tree. 58

Not only is one's body impermanent, but also the whole world system, the universe, is impermanent. The wheel of Saṃsāra continually goes round, characterized by impurity. Further, Saṃsāra is of no benefit, since it is saviourless, without essence, devoid of self, impermanent, and full of suffering. As Āryadeva said in the *Catuḥśataka*,

> How can he, who in this world does not have sorrow, have reverence towards peace (i. e., Nirvāṇa)? Just as it is difficult to part from one's own home so (it is difficult to part from) existence (i. e., Saṃsāra).

Therefore one should think of renouncing the world.

13. The seven suns arise at the end of a great aeon (*mahākalpa*). Each of these aeons is presided over by its own human Buddha.

(2) To make fruitful the opportune conditions through realizing how rare they are

> **O lord of men, make this (human life) fruitful by practising the Holy *Dharma*, for it is more difficult to obtain a human birth from animal states than a tortoise to place (its neck) in the aperture of a wooden yoke which are in the same ocean. 59**

One should think how rare it is to obtain a human birth and the eighteen opportune conditions[14] which are necessary for the practice of Dharma. It is said in *sūtra*, "If the whole universe were an ocean in which there was a yoke being blown by the wind round and round the surface, and on the bottom of this ocean lived a blind tortoise which once every one hundred years came to the surface, still it is more difficult for one to obtain a human birth than it would be for that blind tortoise to place its neck through the opening in that yoke". No example exists which can illustrate the difficulty of obtaining a human life together with the eighteen opportune conditions. Hence human life should not be wasted, but should be used properly.

14. The eighteen opportune conditions which are necessary for the practice of Dharma are:

(1) freedom from the realm of the hells,
(2) freedom from the realm of the hungry ghosts,
(3) freedom from the realm of animals,
(4) freedom from the realm of long-lived gods
(5) freedom from being a heretic,
(6) freedom from being a barbarian,
(7) freedom from being a fool,
(8) freedom from being where there is no teaching from a Buddha,
(9) to have gained a human birth,
(10) to have gained birth in a central realm (where the Saṅgha exists),
(11) possessing sound organs,
(12) to be free from actions which conflict with Dharma,
(13) to have faith in the Holy Dharma,
(14) the advent of a Buddha into the world,
(15) the teaching of the pure religion,
(16) the continuance and stability of the pure religion,
(17) being a believer and follower of the Buddha's teaching, and
(18) having a loving and compassionate heart towards others.

Having obtained a human birth, one who commits sins is more foolish than one who fills a jewel-adorned golden vessel with vomit. 60

There is no greater fool in the world than the one who fails to utilize the opportune conditions which have been obtained. Even among worldly people, one who vomits in a beautiful golden vessel adorned with many jewels is considered a fool. So much more so is one who fails to use a human life and the opportune conditions for the right purpose of attaining liberation. As is said in the *Bodhicaryāvatāra*,

> Having acquired the opportune conditions accordingly, if I do not practise virtue then there is nothing more wasteful or foolish than this.

(3) Counsel to the king to exert himself having achieved an extraordinarily good foundation

You possess the four great conditions : dwelling in a suitable place, relying upon the Holy Ones, having religiously applied yourself in former (lives), and collected merit. 61

In addition to human life and the opportune conditions, there are four special conditions which one can obtain (just as the king) :

(i) birth in a high and noble family so that the Noble Path can be entered upon easily;

(ii) access to holy persons who reduce one's faults and increase one's potentialities;

(iii) freedom from the necessity of toiling for one's food and shelter like others so that Dharma can easily be practised;

(iv) the previous accumulation of immense merit which now gives one the basis (i. e., human life, opportune conditions, and the above three) of treading the path and attaining liberation. Therefore, if one has all the causes for entering the path, then it should be done quickly.

The Sage said that reliance upon a spiritual friend completes the path to holiness. Since very many obtained peace through relying upon the Conqueror, rely on the Holy Ones. 62

Lord Buddha said that since a spiritual friend is the cause for attaining the path to liberation, one should consult him before undertaking anything. This useful and beneficial practice should always be followed. As is said in *Bhagavad-ratnaguṇa-sañcaya-gāthā-pañjikā-nāma*,

> Good disciples who possess reverence for the preceptor should always rely upon learned preceptors, because the knowledge of the learned arises from them and later those (*gurus*) will teach the *Prajñāpāramitā*. The Conqueror who possesses the most excellent of all qualities said, "The qualities of a Buddha are possessed by the spiritual friend".

* * *

Whoever is born as a heretic, animal, hungry ghost, hell being, barbarian, fool, long-lived deity or where there is no teaching from a Buddha, is declared to be born in the eight faulty and unfavourable (states). Having gotten the opportunity to be free from them, then strive to put an end to birth. 63-64

When one is not hindered by any of the conditions contrary to the practice of religion, he should practise *Dharma* without delay. If one is free from the eight faulty states and has the opportune conditions, he should practise religion quickly.

One must renounce Saṃsāra, since it is impermanent and without essence. Having renounced Saṃsāra, one must resolve to practise *Dharma* unceasingly and without hesitation. Further, one should always practise *Dharma* with the steadfast thought of attaining liberation.

B. TO PRODUCE REVULSION FOR SAṂSĀRA

1. *First, in brief*

Grieve over Saṃsāra which is the source of manifold suffering, such as destitution of (what is) desired, death, disease,

old age, etc., and also listen to some of its faults. 65

One should be aware of, and meditate on, the evil consequences of Saṃsāra. The desire for things that one does not have only brings misery. Things that are not wished for occur to one, such as illness, old age, death, etc. One must also remember that even the pleasures of a happy life will result in suffering, such as having to depart from friends, relatives, dear ones, etc. Since Saṃsāra is full of suffering, one should always meditate on renunciation. He who wishes to gain enlightenment must renounce Saṃsāra. Therefore, it is essential to first see existence as suffering. Lord Buddha said, "Understand suffering". One who places his faith in Saṃsāra, which is always full of evil consequences, will have to pay with his own flesh. As is said in the *Catuḥśataka*,

> If there can never be an end to this ocean of suffering, (then) why do you children, sunk in this (ocean), not produce fear ?

2. *Second, the detailed explanation*

a. To consider the uncertainty in Saṃsāra

There are no certainties in Saṃsāra, because fathers become sons, mothers wives, and human enemies friends; likewise, it can happen conversely. 66

Everything is uncertain and insubstantial. In successive lifetimes one's son may later become one's father, etc. Also, one's enemies may become his friends, and one's friends may become his enemies. It is not proper for one to have hatred for his enemies and love for friends. It is wrong to make distinctions among living beings, for at any moment a person may be a friend, and at the next he may be an enemy.

b. To consider dissatisfaction

Everyone has drunk more (mothers') milk than the four oceans; since worldlings follow after the common people, they will have to drink still more than this. 67

Having experienced the pleasures of existence, one desires them again and again and, so, is never satisfied. Each living being has been in Saṃsāra since beginningless time and has thus drunk more mothers' milk than the water contained in the four oceans. Whether one will drink more milk or not depends on oneself alone. One should think about how much more milk he will have to drink if he does not follow the path to liberation but continues to follow the beliefs of the foolish, common people who are bewildered by the darkness of ignorance.

c-d. To lose one's body again and again, and to be born again and again

> **Everyone has had a heap of bones so great as to equal or surpass *Mount Sumeru*; also, the earth will not suffice for counting pills as big as the seeds of a Juniper tree to equal the mothers (one has had).** **68**

One should think of the number of times one has died. If each living being were to collect all the bones he has had from his past existences, then that heap of bones would surpass even Mount Sumeru. So one should think about how many more bones he will collect if he does not follow the path to liberation.

Also, one should think of the number of times one has been born. If one were to count the number of mothers he has had in the past, then that number would be uncountable. Even if one were to make small pills of soil, each as big as a seed, then there would not be enough soil found in the whole world to equal the number of mothers one has had.

e. To consider ascent and descent through the various realms of Saṃsāra

> **Having become *Indra*, deserving the reverence (of) the world, (one) will again fall to the earth on account of the force of (previous) deeds; even having become an universal monarch, (one) will become a servant of a servant in Saṃsāra.** **69**

Sentient beings transmigrate from higher states to lower ones.

The king of the gods, *Indra*, is worshipped by the whole universe. But when his death occurs he will transmigrate to lower states — perhaps even hell — due to his previous bad actions. The universal monarch can also transmigrate into lower states, like that of a servant's servant. One can never be certain of one's position in Saṃsāra.

Having long tasted the happiness of caressing the waists and breasts of the heavenly maidens, once again the very terrible touch of the devices which crush and cut (one's) organs in hell will have to be endured. 70

One can never trust the worldly pleasures of Saṃsāra. One can be born in heaven where he enjoys pleasures, the divine flowers and scents, and the goddesses. However, as a result of past actions one can then be reborn in the burning hells where one is tortured by searing irons. Hence no worldly pleasures can be trusted, nor can it bring lasting happiness, for one can be born into the hells at any time.

Having long dwelt at the summit of *Mount Sumeru* (where one's) feet encounter a comfortable and compliant (surface), consider that again the terrible misery of walking in burning embers and upon decomposed corpses will be experienced. 71

One cannot rely upon the pleasure which results from particular surroundings. One can be born in heaven in a jewelled palace where the ground is composed of gems and one walks in the luxury of softness, etc. Furthermore, all of one's desires are complied with, for when one wants warmth it is given, when one wants cold it is provided, etc. However, the very enjoyments derived from these surroundings can result in the hells where one will have to live in a constantly burning house. Therefore, one cannot depend upon any place in Saṃsāra, for one can find himself anywhere within its realms.

Having reached the beautiful gardens and joyfully played with the heavenly maidens who attend (one), again (one's)

feet, hands, ears and nose will be severed by the sword-like leaves that are in the gardens (of hell). Having entered the celestial maidens' *Mandākinī* River which is endowed with beauty and golden lotuses, once again the salty, difficult to bear and hot *Vaitaraṇī* River will have to be entered. 72-73

One cannot rely upon the pleasure of the heavenly gardens. One can be born in the heavenly gardens where all his wants are satisfied. Yet, again, one can be reborn in hell where the trees have weapon-like leaves which cut one's legs, head, etc. There one will have to experience much suffering.

Having been born in heaven, one plays in the heavenly river, *Mandākinī* (The Leisurely Flowing), and derives much pleasure from playing with the goddesses. But one cannot depend upon these pleasures, because one can be reborn in hell where the river, *Vaitaraṇī* (The Unfordable), is of molten iron. Constantly burned by this liquid, one suffers dreadfully.

Having obtained the very great happiness of the *kāma-dhātu* gods or the dispassionate happiness of *Brahmā*,[15] again the continuous suffering of having become fuel for *Avīci's* fire will have to be endured. Having attained the state of the sun or moon and illuminated the whole world by the light of one's own body, once again having entered into the dense, black darkness one's own outstretched hand will not be seen. 74-75

One should neither rely upon the inferior heavenly pleasures of the *kāma-dhātu* nor the superior heavenly pleasures of the *rūpa-dhātu* and *arūpa-dhātu*. Born in the *rūpa-dhātu*, one is more free than ordinary living beings as a result of his spiritual attainments. Still, as a result of previous bad actions one can be born in the lowest of the hells, *Avīci*, where he will suffer terribly. Even *Brahmā*, who is free from desires as they are known in the

15. *Brahmā* refers to the gods of the *rūpa-dhātu* (realm of form) and *arūpa-dhātu* (formless realm).

kāma-dhātu, can fall from his lofty position and once again experience sufferings.

Having attained the godly state of the sun or moon, one will illumine the whole universe. However, one day one can be born in a region of such darkness that he cannot even see his own body.

Giving, morality and meditation are the real lights that one should take hold of. If one does not have these lights, then he will continue to go from darkness to darkness.

f. To consider one's solitary position

(Since you) will have to suffer thus, take up the bright lamp of the threefold virtue; (otherwise), you alone will have to enter the endless darkness which is not destroyed by sun or moon. 76

Everything is impermanent, so at any moment one may die. One should think that at the time of death he must go alone, without any help from friends or companions. Therefore, if one has the opportunity to practise virtuous deeds of body, voice and mind, then one should do so immediately. As Candrakīrti said in the *Madhyamakāvatāra*,

> If one does not take hold of these (virtues) when one has the requisites and is under his own power, (then) after having fallen into the abyss and come under the power of another, how can one arise ?

One day one will have to go alone and will be faced with many difficulties. At that time, it will be too late for anything to be done. Also, as is said in the *Bodhicaryāvatāra*,

> Though all relatives and friends gather round while I lie on the bed, the feelings of the ceasing of life will be experienced by myself alone. When I have been caught by the messenger of *Yama*, of what benefit are my relatives, of what benefit are my friends. Virtue is the only refuge at that time, but that also was not relied upon by me.

g. To consider the sufferings experienced in the five realms

(1) To consider the suffering in the hells

Living beings who commit offences will always suffer in the hells : *Saṃjīva, Kālasūtra, Pratāpana, Saṃghāta, Raurava, Avīci,* etc. 77

Those living beings who have committed non-virtuous actions through the three doors (i. e., body, speech and mind) will be born in the eight hot hells, thus :

(1) Reviving Hell (Tib. yang. sos., Skt. saṃjīva),
(2) Black Thread Hell (Tib. thig. nag., Skt. kālasūtra),
(3) Crushing Hell (Tib. bsdus. 'joms. Skt. saṃghāta),
(4) Howling Hell (Tib. ngu. 'bod. Skt. raurava),
(5) Great Howling Hell (Tib. ngu. 'bod. chen. po., Skt. mahā-raurava),
(6) Heating Hell (Tib. tsha. ba., Skt. tapana),
(7) Intense Heating Hell (Tib. rab. tu. tsha. ba., Skt. pratāpana),
(8) *Avīci* Hell (Tib. mnar. med., Skt. avīci).

One can also be born into the Cold Hells and the Neighboring Hells.[16] If one is born into these spheres, then the sufferings are long and violent.

There some are pressed like sesamum; similarly, others are ground into fine powder; some are cut by saws; likewise, others are split by the very sharp blades of terrible axes. 78

The Crushing Hell : Born in this hell, one is crushed between two mountains which look like goats' heads. Just as the sesamum

16. The eight Cold Hells are :
(1) Blister Hell (Tib. chu. bar. can., Skt. arbuda),
(2) Bursting Blister Hell (Tib. chu. bar. rdol. pa., Skt. nirarbuda),
(3) 'Brrrr..' Hell (Tib. a. chu. zer. ba., Skt. hahava),
(4) 'Oh..' Hell (Tib. kyi. hud. zer. ba., Skt. huhuva),
(5) Clenched Teeth Hell (Tib. swo. tham. tham. pa., Skt. aṭaṭa),
(6) Blue Lotus Hell (Tib. ut. pal. ltar. gas. pa., Skt. utpala),
(7) Lotus Hell (Tib. pad. ma. ltar. gas. pa., Skt. padma),
(8) Great Lotus Hell (Tib. pad. ma. chen. po. ltar. gas. pa., Skt. mahā padma).
The Neighboring Hells are varied hells of lesser intensity.

is pressed to extract oil, so one is crushed to extract blood. One is also struck with huge hammers, and the like.

The Black Thread Hell : When one is born in this hell, black lines are drawn on one's body along which one is cut with burning saws and axes.

While a burning stream of thick, molten bronze is poured into others, some are completely transfixed by heated barbed-iron spears. 79

The Intense Heating Hell : Only a few examples are given of the many sufferings which are inflicted upon beings in this hell. One's mouth is pried open by a hot poker and is filled with molten iron, burning one's entire body. Spears are also driven from the heels of one's feet through to the crown of his head.

Some with hands outstretched towards the sky are overpowered by fierce dogs with iron fangs; while others, powerless, are torn asunder by ravens with terrible claws and sharp iron beaks. Some, used as food, writhe and utter lamentations when touched by various worms and beetles, flesh-flies and tens of thousands of black bees which cause large terrible wounds. 80-81

Neighboring Hells : In these hells there are many dogs with iron fangs which tear one to pieces. There are also birds with iron beaks which tear out one's eyes. Further, there are many flies, mosquitoes, and other insects which pester, gnaw and eat one.

Again, some with mouths agape are constantly charred in heaps of burning embers; while some, thrust head down, are cooked like a mass of rice in great cauldrons made of iron. 82

One of the Hot Hells : Those in this hell are burnt by fire, or they are boiled in big cauldrons. A special mixture is added so that the parts of one's body separate, and he boils like rice.

Having listened to the measureless suffering of hell, sinners, whose nature is adamant, are not shattered into a thousand pieces; (yet) only the time between the beinnging and end of a breath separates them (from hell). As fear will arise through making images or seeing pictures of hell, reading, remembering or hearing about hell—so if one should experience the terrible consequences, then what need to say anything. 83-84

Having heard about the sufferings which occur in the hells, one should be afraid of them. As the Master Nāgārjuna said on another occasion,

Daily recollect the hot and cold hells.

People who have committed many sins will surely encounter the sufferings of these hells, because the time between the inhaled and the exhaled breath is sufficient for a healthy person to be reborn in hell. If one still does not take notice and become afraid of the hells, then it is strange indeed ! Such a fool, whose heart is as hard as a diamond, cannot be moved by anyone or anything.

If one sees pictures of the hells, or hears about the hells, then this instils much fear. Doing non-virtuous actions will surely cause one to be reborn in one of these hells. Therefore, it is imperative that one avoid non-virtuous actions in order to avoid the hells.

As surely as freedom from attachment produces the most excellent happiness among all happiness, so surely the very dreadful suffering of *Avīci* Hell (is the worst) among all suffering. The sufferings which (one sustains) from violent thrusts by three hundred spears in one day in this world cannot even be compared to a fraction, or a small measure, of hell's suffering. 85-86

Among all the happiness that one can obtain, the best is the one obtained through freedom from desires. Similarly, among all the sufferings that one can experience in Saṃsāra, that of the eighth hot hell, *Avīci*, is the worst.

In this human life, if one's body were pierced by three hundred spears in one day, then that would be a great amount of suffering. In relation to the sufferings experienced in the hells, the pain accrued from those spears is so little that it is of no comparison. As is said in the *Bodhicaryāvatāra*,

> If you possess fear for (the sufferings) of this life like a living fish thrashing (on the sand), (then) what need to say about the unbearable sufferings of hell (which result from) sinful deeds.

* * *

Thus, one will experience very terrible suffering for a hundred million years, for as long as (the force of) those non-virtuous (deeds) is not exhausted, so long will one not be parted from life (in the hells). 87

Living beings will experience the aforementioned sufferings for hundreds of thousands of years. Yet due to continued bad actions, they will continue to suffer indefinitely. This is so because all the results of those evil actions have not yet been manifested. No non-virtuous action performed is lost, and the full results of those deeds will be borne by oneself alone. As is said in the *Samādhirāja Sūtra*,

> Having also committed sin, it will not be not felt (by you), and (sin) committed by another will not be felt (by you).

* * *

Therefore, by your own skill try not to acquire even an atom of fault—the seed of these fruits of non-virtue—through your conduct of body, speech and mind. 88

The sufferings described above result from non-virtuous actions committed through the three doors of body, speech and mind. So people should avoid the slightest non-virtuous action in all possible ways and at all times. As *rgyal. sras. thogs. med.* said,

The Sage said that the suffering of the states of woe (which is) difficult to bear is the result of sinful deeds. So the practice of the Bodhisattva is never to do sinful deeds even if death threatens.

(2) To consider the suffering of animals

Those who abandon the virtue resulting in peace (will be born) in animal realms where there are also various dreadful sufferings, such as : eating one another, killing, binding, beating, etc. 89

Having been born an animal, one must go about with lowered head. One is beaten, used, maltreated and killed. There are many kinds of suffering. and one is absolutely ignorant of virtuous actions which are the principal corrective for avoiding these kinds of sufferings.

Some are killed for pearls, wool, bones, meat, or skin; while others, powerless, are employed by kicking, striking, whipping or prodding with iron hooks. 90

Some animals are killed for pearls, hair, bones, meat, and the like. The desirable things which they naturally possess are not free for their own use. They will lose their lives since people also desire them. Some animals are beaten, others are hooked, and still others are caged — all of which cause great suffering. On another occasion Ācārya Nāgārjuna said,

Look upon animals (who have) very many sufferings (resulting) from stupidity and recollect (those sufferings).

(3) To consider the suffering of hungry ghosts

Also among hungry ghosts continuous, unallayed suffering is produced through the lack of desired objects. Very terrible (sufferings) created by fear, hunger, thirst, cold, heat and weariness will have to be endured. 91

Not only is there much suffering and pain in the hell and animal realms, but also in this third realm of the hungry ghosts. The suffering experienced by the hungry ghosts is a result of their having been miserly during former existences. As a result of this, they undergo the hardships resulting from extreme temperatures, hunger, thirst, and the like. In order to obtain food, they run here and there with many hardships, and usually with no success. If, by chance, they come upon some desirable food, then frightful, weapon-bearing creatures appear and assault them.

Some, troubled by hunger, are not even able to eat a little discarded, coarse, or foul (food), (for each has) a mouth as big as the eye of a needle and a stomach the size of a mountain. 92

Some hungry ghosts have a very small mouth which is no larger than the eye of a needle. They have a throat as thin as a hair, but a stomach as big as a mountain. For this reason, they are always miserable. Even if they should find some very filthy food, still it is difficult for it to enter their mouths. Then, if they manage to get it into their mouths, it is still more difficult for it to pass through their throats. Finally, if it should pass through their throats, then their stomachs are so huge that it is of no consequence.

Some, like the upper reaches of a dried palmyra tree, are naked with bodies of skin and bones; while some, with flames nightly (issuing) from (their) mouths, devour food of burning sand which has fallen into (their) mouths. 93

Some hungry ghosts, devoid of flesh and blood, are very thin. As they are only skin and bones, they look like dried palmyra trees. Not only are they unable to find food, but occasionally fire issues from their mouths. Even should they find a small amount of food, having eaten it, it turns into fire and burns their bodies. As a result they suffer very much.

Some poor ones cannot even find impure (food) like pus, excrement, blood, etc., so, striking one another's face, (they)

eat the pus of ripened goitres growing from (their) throats. 94

These hungry ghosts have the least merit. They search in every direction for food, but they never find desirable food. Occasionally they may find unwholesome food like pus, vomit, etc., but they fight one another even for this. At other times they fight each other for the pus from goitres which grow on their companions' throats.

For them even the moon is hot in the summertime, while even the sun is cold in the winter; trees become fruitless and rivers dry up if only looked upon by them. 95

The conditions for hungry ghosts are generally as follows. In the summertime the moon is hot, and in the wintertime the sun is cold for them. Since they possess so little merit, if they look upon a tree bearing beautiful fruit, then that tree becomes dry, fruitless, ugly, and useless. Again, beautiful rivers become dry and sandy if looked upon by hungry ghosts.

Having endured uninterrupted suffering, some individuals—securely bound by the noose of evil deeds committed—will not die for five or even ten thousand years. 96

Hungry ghosts are very securely bound by the rope of their former deeds. They always suffer from hunger and thirst. They must undergo these kinds of sufferings constantly for at least five or ten thousand years. As the Master Nāgārjuna said on another occasion,

> Also remember hungry ghosts (who are) emaciated by hunger and thirst.

* * *

The Buddha said, "Though the sufferings which are experienced by hungry ghosts are various, they are of one taste; the cause is the avarice, miserliness and ignobility of people." 97

As said before, the sufferings of hungry ghosts are hunger, thirst, cold, heat, weariness, etc. These kinds of sufferings are the result of miserliness which they practised while alive as human beings. Wealthy people who are avaricious, who do not offer, who do not give, who do not even eat, who are always thinking of accumulating more and more, are thus born as hungry ghosts. Even after the suffering in the realm of hungry ghosts has ended, if they happen to be born among men, then they will be very poor. As is said in the *Ārya-prajñāpāramitā-sañcaya-gāthā*,

> One who is miserly will be born in the state of hungry ghosts; even if by chance he be born in the human (realm), at that time he will be poor.

So to be rich in a future life, one must give liberally.

(4) To consider the suffering of gods

Also, (as a result) of the great pleasures in the heavens, the suffering of death and transmigration is greater; having contemplated thus, nobles should not crave for heaven which will come to an end. 98

In the higher realm of the *kāma-dhātu* gods, one has great wealth, pleasure and happiness. The gods have so much happiness that they never think of death. However, their happiness is not permanent. At the time of their approaching death, they experience great mental anguish. Since they know the sufferings which will befall them in the near future, their suffering is even greater than the physical sufferings of the hells.

As is said in the *Saṃbhāraparikathā*,

> In whatever manner he strives, still (a god) will not live long; like a bird soaring in the sky and an arrow shot with the strength of a child, is he destined to fall.

So if one is intelligent and wise, then he will not seek happiness in the higher realms — like those of the gods. The realm of the gods is without essence and impermanent, so one must abandon attachment to this kind of happiness.

> **Their bodies' complexion becomes ugly, they do not like to sit, their garlands of flowers wither, their clothes become soiled, and sweat appears on their bodies—(all of which) never happened before. Just as on earth the signs of dying foretell man's approaching death, so these five former signs presage the death and transmigration of the gods dwelling in heaven.** **99-100**

As the signs of death come to human beings, so do they come to the gods. When the time comes for a god to die, these five signs appear.

(1) Though they are usually very beautiful, they lose their great beauty and become very ugly.

(2) Though they are ordinarily never bored because of their many pleasures, they become bored and do not know what to do.

(3) Though their bodies are normally adorned with flowers which never wither, now they wither and die.

(4) Though their clothes are normally clean and beautiful, now they become soiled and dirty.

(5) Though their bodies are usually never unclean or sweaty, now they are.

At that time the gods know that they are about to die, and they realize that they have never thought about religion. They see the lower realms — like the hells — into which they will fall and the sufferings that will shortly befall them, so they experience unbearable mental suffering.

> **If there is not any merit remaining when transmigrating from the worlds of the gods, then, powerless, (they) will dwell as either animals, hungry ghosts or denizens of hell.** **101**

The gods will transmigrate from higher realms to lower ones. Having no choice, they must leave their beautiful abode. They will suffer greatly because of having formerly enjoyed such a beautiful and pleasurable state. Their suffering will be even greater than those of others. Excluding the hells, living beings who inhabit the other realms become accustomed to their suffering. However, the suffering of the gods is still greater because of having lived in a world of pleasure.

(5) To consider the suffering of demigods

Also among the demigods, there is great mental suffering because of natural hostility toward the splendor of the gods; though they are also intelligent the truth is not seen due to the veil of (their) *Karma*.[17] 102

There is inherent mental suffering in the realm of the demigods. The demigods are always envious of the gods, because they cannot equal their wealth and splendor. For this reason, they always war with the gods. Yet when they battle with the gods, they suffer very much through being speared, etc. Although they are wiser than men, they are so thoroughly bound by this strife that they are unable to realize any truth in their lives.

3. *To establish the understanding of Saṃsāra as unfortunate*

Saṃsāra is thus (as explained above), so birth is unfortunate among gods, men, denizens of hell, hungry ghosts, and animals. Realize that birth is a receptacle of many ills. 103

As seen from the above, it is unfortunate to be born in any of the six realms. Reflecting upon this, one should become frightened. One should be afraid that he will be born in these realms as a result of deeds and the defilements. So one must realize that Saṃsāra is really dreadful. One should completely free oneself from Saṃsāra so as not to be born there again.

17. Tib. 'gro. ba., Skt. vipāka, literally means the ripened results of former actions.

C. TO CONSIDER THE EXCELLENT QUALITIES OF NIRVĀṆA AND PRACTISE THE PATH RESULTING IN NIRVĀṆA

1. *General counsel with respect to all the disciplines which result in Nirvāṇa*

a. To strive to attain Nirvāṇa

(As you would) extinguish a fire if it suddenly caught hold of your clothes or head, just so strive to put an end to rebirth through renouncing deeds—for there is no other aim more excellent than this. 104

Attaining Nirvāṇa is a lengthy process, so one should begin as quickly as possible. If one's head or clothes were to catch fire, then one would immediately extinguish it. Similarly, one should try his utmost to put an end to rebirth in Saṃsāra which is the result of deeds and defilements. To put an end to rebirth in Saṃsāra which should be known to be the root of all ills, one should practise the Path, for there is nothing more excellent.

Through morality, wisdom and concentration gain the peaceful, subdued and untainted state of Nirvāṇa which is ageless, deathless, inexhaustible, and devoid of earth, water, fire, air, sun and moon. 105

(i) morality (Tib. tshul.khrims., Skt. śila)
(ii) wisdom (Tib. shes. rab., Skt. prajñā)
(iii) concentration (Tib. bsam. gtan., Skt. dhyāna)

Through practising these three, which are the principal causes for attaining Nirvāṇa, one will achieve peace. Nirvāṇa is of two kinds. The first is called Nirvāṇa without substratum, without the five aggregates, final Nirvāṇa, i.e., *nirupādhiśeṣanirvāṇa.* The second is called Nirvāṇa with substratum, i.e., *sopādhiśeṣa-nirvāṇa*; that is, with the five aggregates though their emptiness (*śūnyatā*) is realized.

The first is free from the aggregates which have been exhausted and extinguished. One attains the peace of Nirvāṇa. The second involves the realization of *śūnyatā*; though one still possesses the aggregates, they will be left behind at the time of death.

Both are called pure and clear, because the defilements have been vanquished. From this time forth, there is no aging, so it is called ageless. It is also called immortal, because there is no more death. It is inexhaustible, colorless and shapeless. The state which one will attain is devoid of the four elements, the sun and moon. This is said because in some Hindu philosophies the goal is the union of the elements, and the sun and moon, etc. In order to show that liberation is formless, this has been said.

Furthermore, both Nirvāṇas are free from thought activity, conceptualization and distraction.

b. Counsel to accumulate that which is needed to attain Nirvāṇa

(1) To practise the seven branches of enlightenment

These seven limbs of enlightenment—mindfulness, discrimination of things (*dharmas*), energy, joy, purification, trance, and evenmindedness—are the accumulation of virtue which is the cause of obtaining Nirvāṇa. 106

There are seven special parts to the path to liberation which are called the seven limbs of enlightenment.

(1) Mindfulness which does not forget the vision of the truth is the limb of dwelling at the level of the first *bhūmi.*

(2) Wisdom which discriminates *dharmas* in the limb of intrinsic character.

(3) Energy which gives rise to virtuous actions is the limb of deliverance.

(4) Joy which is the happiness of mind resulting from realization is the limb of benefit and merit.

(5) Purification which corrects actions of body and mind is the limb of avoidance of anything tainted by the defilements.

(6) Transic states which is the possession of a clear and meditative mind is the limb of the non-arising of the defilements.

(7) Evenmindedness which is free from sleepiness and distraction is the limb of non-involvement with any defilement.

These seven parts of the path to enlightenment are causes of attaining Nirvāṇa.

(2) To indicate that Nirvāṇa is attained through the combination of quietude and insight

> **Without wisdom there is no concentration, and, again, without concentration there is no wisdom; but for one who has these two, the ocean of existence is made to be like (the water in) a cow's hoof-print. 107**

(i) concentration (i.e., here in the sense of quietude; Tib. bsam.gtan., Skt. dhyāna)

(ii) wisdom (i.e., here in the sense of insight; Tib. shes.rab., Skt. prajñā)

Without wisdom one cannot have correct concentration. This is because all 'worldly' and 'transcendent qualities' are attained through wisdom. As Ācārya Nāgārjuna said,

> Wisdom is the root of all these seen and unseen[18] qualities; therefore one must hold wisdom completely in order to attain both.

Conversely, without concentration one cannot have wisdom. This wisdom is the understanding of emptiness (*śūnyatā*).

Before one can have wisdom, one must have both mental and physical tranquility which are achieved through concentration. That is, one must have the foundation of concentration in order to obtain the realization of *śūnyatā*. Any *yogin* who has both correct concentration and wisdom makes the whole ocean of Saṃsāra dry up very quickly — like the water in a cow's hoof-print in the mud. The person who has both concentration and wisdom jointly is able to get rid of the root of Saṃsāra.

Principally one must meditate on wisdom. Though one may

18. Here 'seen' and 'unseen' refer to this life and the next respectively.

have many other wonderful qualities, unless one has the true understanding of *śūnyatā* one will never be able to relinquish the cause of Saṃsāra. The root of Samsāra is clinging. As it is said in the *Samādhirāja Sūtra*,

> Worldly people cannot destroy the perception of self even though they meditate transic states. After (meditating thus) again (their minds) are agitated by defilements just as (occurred when) Adhicaryā meditated transic states. If one investigates, without self, upon *dharmas* and then meditates on that which was investigated, (then) this will be the cause of the fruit of obtaining Nirvāṇa (and) any cause other than this will not produce peace.

(3) To reject speculation upon that which is inexpressible

These fourteen pronouncements which were declared by the Kinsman of the Sun to be inexpressible in the world are not conducive to peace of mind, so do not speculate upon them. **108**

One should not dwell upon the fourteen erroneous views. These fourteen are like a net which further entangles one in the defilements. These views are not conducive to one's release from Saṃsāra as they obstruct one's path to Nirvāṇa. These are the fourteen questions asked to, and unanswered by, the Kinsman of the Sun (i.e., Lord Buddha).

(1) Whether the universe is (a) eternal, (b) not eternal, (c) both eternal and not eternal, and (d) neither eternal nor not eternal.

(2) Whether the universe is (a) finite, (b) infinite, (c) both finite and infinite, and (d) neither finite nor infinite.

(3) Whether the *Tathāgata* (a) exists after death, (b) does not exist after death, (c) both exist after death and do not exist after death, and (d) neither exists after death nor does not exist after death.

(4) Whether the soul is identical with the body or different from it.

Lord Buddha declined to answer these questions, because they are not well founded. A question does not merit an answer if the object of the query does not really exist. For instance, if one were to ask, "What is the size of the house on the planet Venus?"

(4) To understand Interdependent Origination which frees one from Saṃsāra

The Sage declared, "From ignorance originate predispositions, from the latter consciousness, from consciousness originate name and form, from name and form originate the six sense-organs, from the sense-organs contact, from contact originates feeling, from the foundation of feeling originates craving, from craving grasping, from grasping originates becoming, from becoming birth occurs—if there is birth, then a very great heap of sufferings ensues, such as sorrow, disease, old age, frustration, fear of death, etc.; however, by putting an end to birth, all these will cease."
109-111

If there is ignorance, grasping of a self, then one is subject to all the miseries of existence and continually circles in Saṃsāra. From this ignorance, predispositions arise. (These two are causes pertaining to former existences which give to the present life.) From predispositions, consciousness arises. From consciousness, name and form are produced. From name and form, the six inner sense spheres originate. From these, contact between the sense-organs and their objects is produced. From contact, pleasant, unpleasant, etc., feelings arise. From the foundation of feeling, there arises craving which is the desire for happiness and the aversion to suffering. From craving, grasping ensues. From grasping, becoming is produced. (These eight are conditions of the present life which result in rebirth). From becoming, birth is engendered. If there is birth, then old age, sickness, death, and the like arise. (These two are conditions pertaining to the subsequent life.)

Suffering arises again and again from this combination of

causes. But if one could put an end to rebirth in Saṃsāra which results from deeds and defilements, then all the sufferings of disease, old age and death would cease. If one is not born in Saṃsāra, then one is free from becoming. When becoming is stopped, birth ceases. When birth is stopped, the twelve links from ignorance up to old age and death are extinguished. In this way one should investigate and meditate upon this Interdependent Origination endowed with twelve links which leads either to Saṃsāra or Nirvāṇa. Therefore one should produce a complete renunciation of Saṃsāra. The root of Saṃsāra is ignorance, the grasping of a self, and the opposite of this is the Truth, *Śūnyatā*. Having produced the realization of *Śūnyatā*, which is the profound natural state of all things, through meditating upon the twelve links of Interdependent Origination, one will surely achieve the pure state of liberation.

Lord Buddha said that one who understands the twelve links of Interdependent Origination will understand Saṃsāra and Nirvāṇa. Both of these are only an illusion of mind which is, itself, empty.

This (doctrine of) Interdependent Origination is the profound and precious treasure of the teaching of the Conqueror; one who rightly sees this (Interdependent Origination) sees the most excellent Buddha, the Knower of Reality. 112

Though all things in this ocean of existence are ultimately not existent — for in reality not even an atom exists — nevertheless phenomena as they appear and are experienced (i.e., things arisen from causes and conditions) are not denied. As the teaching of Interdependent Origination demonstrates, all things are dependent on others for their existence (that is, all things are devoid of own-being).

One must remember that all conditioned things (i.e., things which are interdependently originated) are not different from the Ultimate Truth, and, at the same time, the Ultimate Truth is not different from them. People are bound in Saṃsāra by the defilements and thought constructions, because they do not realize the truth.

So long as one continues to cling to the five aggregates, one has an ego or the grasping of a self. This grasping of a self leads one to perform actions which, in turn, cause one to continue to be born in the round of Saṃsāric existence.

With the realization of *śūnyatā* (emptiness), all defilements and thought constructions will automatically cease. This is because, at the time of realization, one will see that there is no self, no other, no time, etc. Therefore when actions and the grasping of a self cease, one is free from Saṃsāra.

There is no better method for attaining liberation than the realization of *śūnyatā* (i.e., insubstantiality of the self and the insubstantiality of the elements of existence). Clinging to the extreme views of eternalism, nihilism, and the like, will cease when this realization is produced, and only the 'middle way' of the Madhyamaka will remain. As Lord Buddha, who is the only one who can explain this, said, "Everything is Interdependent Origination." Therefore, Interdependent Origination is the real essence of Lord Buddha's teaching, because one cannot say that any thing which he perceives is: (i) born from itself, (ii) born from others, (iii) born from both, and (iv) born without a cause. This is not a rejection of *dharmas* (things) as they are seen, but the Ultimate Truth is something of a different order.

(i) Some say that a thing is born from itself. However, the fault of this contention lies in the fact of its change. A thing which changes cannot, itself, be said to be identical. For example, a sprout is not the same as the seed. Further, if a thing is born from itself, then its origination would be a needless repetition as it is already existent. Further, if a thing were born from itself, then it would reproduce itself *ad infinitum* as there would be nothing to prevent its endless self-reproduction.

(ii) Alternatively, some say that a thing is born from another. However, the fault of this contention lies in the fact that, if this were so, anything could be born from anything. For example, a wheat sprout could be produced from a rice seed.

(iii) Some say that a thing is born from both itself and another. However, this contention contains the faults of both the preceding positions.

(iv) Some say that a thing is born neither from itself nor

from another, i.e., by chance. However, nothing can be born without cause.

As Ācārya Nāgārjuna writes in the opening verse of the *Mūlamadhyamakakārikā*,

> Never are any existing things found to originate from themselves, from others, from both, or without cause.

In this manner, one is not able to say that anything originates. Only through the conjunction of causes and conditions is a result made manifest. Only apparently are things seen to originate. The cause and the result are dependent one upon the other. Neither of them can be grasped as real in its own-being, so they are interdependently originated. Everything that is seen is like the reflection of the moon in water, therefore it can neither be said that it is existent nor non-existent. Since beginningless time all external and internal *dharmas* cannot be said to be real. However, at the same time, *śūnyatā* cannot be said to be different from the phenomenal world. As the *Prajñāpāramitā Hṛdaya Sūtra* states,

> Form is emptiness, emptiness is form, emptiness is also not different from form, form is not different from emptiness....

Therefore, the doctrine of Interdependent Origination, taught by Lord Buddha, is said to be the most precious teaching (*dharma*).

As this doctrine is extremely profound and difficult to understand, one should familiarize oneself with it, study it, and contemplate it with a clear mind. Those who understand the 'twelve links of Interdependent Origination' see the truth. As is said in the *Ārya-prajñāpāramitā-sañcaya-gāthā*,

> The Bodhisattva — who through understanding the wisdom of Interdependent Origination which is non-produced and non-exhausted destroys the darkness of ignorance as the rays of the sun free from clouds

spread forth destroying darkness — will attain enlightenment.

(5) To meditate on the Noble Eightfold Path

In order to attain peace practise these eight parts of the Path: right view, right livelihood, right effort, right mindfulness, right trance, right speech, right action, and right thought. 113

Right view is the limb which investigates completely. Right thought is the limb which makes other things known. Right livelihood, speech and action are the limbs which cause others to have faith. Right mindfulness, trance and effort are the limbs which are the correctives of the various defilements. These are the eight branches of the path. One must practise this Noble Eightfold Path in order to attain the state of Nirvāṇa which is peace.

(6) To consider the Four Noble Truths

This birth is suffering; craving is called the great source of that (suffering); its cessation is liberation; and the path to attain that (liberation) is the Noble Eightfold Path. So in this way, always try to realize the Four Noble Truths, for even laymen dwelling in the lap of prosperity cross the river of the defilements by this knowledge. 114-115

(i) The First Truth; One is subject to birth and death because of deeds and the defilements, so one always circles in Saṃsāra. One experiences suffering resulting from the five aggregates. This is called the Truth of Suffering.

(ii) The Second Truth : Clinging to the five aggregates is the cause of suffering. This is the source of all pain. This is called the Truth of Origination.

(iii) The Third Truth : The third is the Truth of Cessation which is characterized by the extinction of all suffering. This is also called the Truth of Liberation.

(iv) The Fourth Truth : To attain Nirvāṇa, one must practise and follow the Noble Eightfold Path which has been described. This is the Truth of the Path.

The Four Noble Truths are true for the Holy Ones (*āryans*), but are not true for worldlings. Hence the Four Noble Truths should be understood rightly.

Understanding Saṃsāra to be full of suffering, one must think of its bad consequences no matter where one is born. Having truly understood that all of Saṃsāra is suffering, one will then desire liberation which is free from suffering. This will cause one to become interested in entering the Path of Dharma. Firstly, one should think that one's five aggregates are impermanent. Secondly, one should think that generally all of Saṃsāra, especially the place where one is situated, is full of suffering. At the same time, one should think that there is no creator of suffering and that the nature of suffering is *śūnyatā*. In reality, he who experiences suffering does not exist. One should then think how suffering arises — thus from deeds and the defilements. Then one will desire to relinquish the cause of suffering. Thereafter, the Truth of Cessation should be realized. Finally, one should practise the Path, and especially the meditation on *śūnyatā*. One should practise the Four Noble Truths in this way. As Lord Buddha said,

> One should understand suffering, one should remove the cause, one should realize the cessation of suffering, one should practise the Path.

Again, it is said in the *Uttaratantra*

> Suffering, its cause, its cessation and likewise the Path; understand (which are to be) known and (which are to be) rejected and adhere to (the former).

If one really practises in this way, there is no doubt that he will attain Nirvāṇa. In ancient times, a barbarian king saw a picture of Lord Buddha, saw the wheel of life, understood the 'twelve links of Interdependent Origination' with its forward and backward motion, understood the Four Noble Truths, and thus crossed the ocean of Saṃsāra. If one understands these, just as the ancient king, then one will also cross the ocean of Saṃsāra.

(7) Not to hesitate to strive for Nirvāṇa

Those who realized the Truth neither fell from the sky nor sprang up from the womb of the earth like grain, as they were formerly persons subject to the defilements. 116

The Holy Ones have vanquished the first two Truths and are possessed of the second two. They did not possess the Truth from the very beginning. They did not fall from the sky or spring up from the earth possessing the Truth innately, but realized it through their own efforts. They suffered and were subject to the defilements just the same as anyone else. However, they consulted spiritual guides, performed the right actions, practised the Path, and finally attained an enlightened state. So one should not be discouraged, but continually practise. As is said in the *Bodhicaryāvatāra,*

> Having been born a man of a race like me, having recognized benefit and harm, if (I) do not forsake the enlightened conduct, why should I not attain Enlightenment ?

(8) Counsel in brief

O fearless one, the Blessed One said that the mind is the root of virtue, so discipline your mind; this is beneficial and useful advice, so what need to say more. 117

The most beneficial practice for temporal and final results is as follows. Thus far one has been unable to control his own mind, but has, on the contrary, been controlled by his mind. One's mind, in turn, has been subject to the many defilements. Due to this, one has accumulated many actions. Therefore, one has never been free from Saṃsāra, but has always circled through birth and death. So now, one must control his own mind

ĀRYA AVALOKITESHVARA

and always carefully avoid the defilements and non-virtuous ways. Thus one should discipline his mind with care. If one does this, he will accumulate a great heap of virtue. Lord Buddha said that the root of all virtues is to discipline one's own mind. Again, as is said in the *Bodhicaryāvatāra*,

> By that method my mind should be well-held and well-protected; what is the use of much asceticism except the practice of guarding the mind.

* * *

It is difficult even for a monk in isolation to follow the counsel which has been given to you: (yet) make this life meaningful through cultivating the quality of the essence of any of these practices. 118

One should try to follow all of the instructions described in this letter. However, even for a monk living alone in the forest who has no other duties to perform, it is difficult to follow all of these. Certainly the person of family life who has many other obligations will find it extremely difficult. However, one should perform whichever of these practices he can, such as avoiding non-virtuous actions, performing virtuous actions, etc. In this way, one's life will be purposeful, useful, and not wasted. Through practising in this way, one will gain the higher realms, and there is no doubt that one will eventually gain enlightenment. As is said in Ārya Nāgārjuna's *Ratnāvalī*,

> Firstly, Dharma results in prosperity and happiness; later liberation. By the reason of having obtained prosperity and happiness, liberation will gradually arise.

2. *Counsel to practise the Path of the Mahāyāna*

a. To enter the Mahāyāna Path through rejoicing in the demonstration of the *Dharma*.

Having rejoiced in the virtues of all (living beings), having also dedicated your threefold good conduct to the attainment

of Buddhahood, and having mastered the whole of yoga, then you will have countless births in the realms of gods and men through this heap of merit. 119-120a

The Buddhas and Bodhisattvas always rejoice in all the virtuous actions done by both Holy Ones and common people. Similarly, the merit of all virtuous actions that one performs through body, speech and mind should always be dedicated. For instance, one should think as follows, "By the merit of this action, may all sentient beings attain enlightenment." As is said in the *Bodhicaryāvatāra*,

> Do not perform (actions) whether seen or unseen except for the sake of others; dedicate all (virtues) only for the sake of (other) living beings in order that (they attain) enlightenment.

If one dedicates his merits to the good of all sentient beings, one will have many, many auspicious births that are required for the attainment of enlightenment. Also, through mastering the whole of yoga which includes quietude, insight, trance, and the like, one will acquire measureless qualities which will enable him to perceive the Truth.

Born (like) Ārya Avalokiteśvara aiding through (his) conduct many stricken people and dispelling disease, old age, attachment and hatred, dwell for limitless lifetimes like the Protector of the World, the Blessed One Amitābha in His Buddha-field. 120b-121

Through the power of virtuous actions one has done, one should try to be as Ārya Avalokiteśvara who, since ancient times, through his body, speech and mind has helped so many distressed sentient beings and placed them on the right path. Thus born in Saṃsāra, one should help all sentient beings to vanquish suffering and its cause and mature them so that thev may enter the right path.

Through the power of virtuous actions one has performed one

BUDDHA AMITĀBHA

should have the intention, even from this moment, to help all sentient beings attain liberation —just as the Buddha Amitābha who is the Great Saviour of living beings. One day one will become like the Buddha Amitābha who, for as long as Saṃsāra exists, dwells in His Buddha-field[19] for the purpose of only helping all sentient beings to attain enlightenment. As Śāntideva said in the *Bodhicaryāvatāra*,

> As long as space exists and as long as living beings exist, so long may I remain in order to remove the sufferings of living beings

b. To attain Nirvāṇa having gained Buddhahood and having accomplished the benefit of living beings.

> **Having spread to the gods' realms, the sky and on the earth (your) great unblemished fame arising from wisdom, morality and giving, having surely subdued the delight of gods in heaven and men on earth in the enjoyment of excellent maidens, and having gained the Lordship of the Conquerors extinguishing the arising of fear and death for multitudes of living beings afflicted by the defilements, attain the faultless, ageless, fearless state (which is) peaceful, only nominal, and transcendent. 122-123**

One must now properly possess the wisdom which distinguishes between the phenomenal and the ultimate. Also, one must observe the moral discipline which was pledged to the Gurus. At the time of giving, one should apprehend neither the gift, the recipient nor the giver, and one must practise giving with absolutely no attachment to his own life and property. Through these practices, one will gain immense fame which will spread to the realms of the gods, and to all the corners of the earth where men dwell. Hearing of this fame, all living beings will turn away from their attachments and will think of renunciation because of boredom with, and distaste for, what they have been

19. The Buddha-field of the Buddha Amitābha is called the Happy Land (Skt. Sukhāvatī, Tib. bde. ba. can.).

doing with their lives. That is, one will help to destroy the sufferings of all living beings who are subject to the defilements and so save them from rebirth in Saṃsāra which results from deeds and the defilements.

One will attain the enlightenment of a Buddha who forever saves sentient beings from suffering. As is said in the *Ārya-mahāpratihārya-nirdeśa-nāma-mahāyāna-sūtra*

> Having abandoned one's kingdom as one expels spittle, having gone to and resided in a lonely, solitary place, having abandoned the defilements and destroyed *Māra*, there one will become a perfected Buddha — enlightened, stainless and uncompounded.

The Buddhahood which one will attain is endowed with every transcendent quality. However, Buddhahood is, in its own-being, not existent, because in reality its nature is *śūnyatā* which is beyond qualities, beyond the extremes of existence and non-existence, beyond activities, beyond thought, and beyond expression. Hence it is only a name. It is said to be fearless because it is free from threats and fears. It is said that it is ageless, because it is free from death and any kind of impermanence. Moreover, it is inexhaustible. Through attaining this Great Nirvāṇa, one will become the Saviour and Protector of all sentient beings.

BUDDHA SHĀKYAMUNI

APPENDIX I

༄། །སློབ་དཔོན་ཀླུ་སྒྲུབ་ཀྱི་བཤེས་པའི་སྤྲིངས་ཡིག་
བཞུགས་སོ།།

༄༅། །རྒྱ་གར་སྐད་དུ། སུ་ཧྲི་ད་ལེ་ཁ།
བོད་སྐད་དུ། བཤེས་པའི་སྤྲིངས་ཡིག།

འཇམ་དཔལ་གཞོན་ནུར་གྱུར་པ་ལ་ཕྱག་འཚལ་ལོ།

ཡོན་ཏན་རང་བཞིན་དགེ་འོས་བདག་གིས་ནི།
བདེ་བར་གཤེགས་པའི་གསུང་བསྒྲད་ལས་བྱུང་བའི།
བསོད་ནམས་འདུན་སླད་འཕགས་པའི་དབྱངས་འདི་དག།
ཕུང་ཟད་ཅིག་བསྒྲུབས་ཁྱོད་ཀྱིས་གསན་པའི་རིགས།། ༡ །།

ཇི་ལྟར་བདེ་གཤེགས་སྐུ་གཟུགས་ཤིང་ལས་ཀྱང་།
བགྱིས་པ་ཅི་འདྲའང་རུང་སྟེ་མཁས་པས་མཆོད།
དེ་བཞིན་བདག་གི་སྙན་ངག་འདི་ངན་ཡང་།
དམ་ཆོས་བརྗོད་ལ་བརྟེན་སླད་སྨད་མི་བགྱི།། ༢ །།

ཐུབ་པ་ཆེན་པོའི་བཀའ་ནི་སྙན་དགུ་ཞིག།
ཁྱོད་ཀྱི་ཐུགས་སུ་ལྷ་ཡང་ཆུད་མོད་ཀྱི།
རྗོ་ཐལ་ལས་བགྱིས་དགུང་ཟླའི་འོད་ཀྱིས་ནི།
ཆེས་དཀར་ཉིད་དུ་ཅི་སྟེ་མི་འགྱུར་ལགས།། ༣ །།

རྒྱལ་བས་སངས་རྒྱས་ཆོས་དང་དགེ་འདུན་དང་།
གཏོང་དང་ཚུལ་ཁྲིམས་ལྷ་རྗེས་དྲན་པ་དྲུག།
རབ་ཏུ་བཀའ་སྩལ་དེ་དག་སོ་སོ་ཡི།
ཡོན་ཏན་ཚོགས་ཀྱིས་རྗེས་སུ་དྲན་པར་བགྱི།། ༤ །།

དགེ་བའི་ལས་ལམ་བཅུ་པོ་ལུས་དང་ནི།
ངག་དང་ཡིད་ཀྱིས་རྟག་ཏུ་བསྟེན་བགྱི་ཞིང་།
ཆང་རྣམས་ལས་ལྡོག་དེ་བཞིན་དགེ་བ་ཡི།
འཚོ་བ་ལ་ཡང་མངོན་པར་དགེས་པར་མཛོད།། ༥ །།

ཡོངས་སྤྱོད་གཡོ་བ་སྙིང་པོ་མེད་མཁྱེན་ནས།
དགེ་སློང་བྲམ་ཟེ་བཀྲེན་དང་བཤེས་རྣམས་ལ།
སྦྱིན་པ་ཚུལ་བཞིན་སྩོལ་བགྱི་ཕ་རོལ་ཏུ།
སྦྱིན་ལས་གཞན་པའི་གཉེན་མཆོག་མ་མཆིས་སོ།། ༤།།

ཁྱོད་ཀྱིས་ཚུལ་ཁྲིམས་མ་ཉམས་སྨོད་མི་དམའ།
མ་འདྲེས་མ་སྦགས་པ་དག་བསྟེན་པར་མཛོད།
ཁྲིམས་ནི་རྒྱུ་དང་མི་རྒྱུའི་ས་བཞིན་དུ།
ཡོན་ཏན་ཀུན་གྱི་གཞི་རྟེན་ལགས་པར་གསུངས།། ༥།།

སྦྱིན་དང་ཚུལ་ཁྲིམས་བཟོད་བརྩོན་བསམ་གཏན་དང་།
དེ་བཞིན་ཤེས་རབ་གཞལ་མེད་ཕ་རོལ་ཕྱིན།
འདི་དག་རྒྱས་མཛོད་སྲིད་པའི་རྒྱ་མཚོ་ཡི།
ཕ་རོལ་ཕྱིན་པ་རྒྱལ་བའི་དབང་པོར་མཛོད།། ༦།།

གང་ལ་ཕ་དང་མ་དག་མཆོད་པ་ཡི།
རིགས་དེ་ཚངས་བཅས་སློབ་དཔོན་བཅས་པ་ལགས།
དེ་དག་ལ་མཆོད་གྲགས་པར་འགྱུར་བ་དང་།
ཕྱིད་མ་ལ་ཡང་མཐོ་རིས་འགྱུར་བ་ལགས།། ༩ །།

འཚེ་དང་ཆོམ་རྐུན་འཁྲིག་པ་བརྫུན་དང་ནི།
ཆང་དང་དུས་མིན་ཟས་ལ་ཆགས་པ་དང་།
མལ་སྟན་མཐོ་ལ་དགའ་དང་གླུ་དག་དང་།
གར་དང་འཕྲེང་བའི་ཁྱད་པར་རྣམས་སྤང་ཞིང་།། ༡༠ །།

དགྲ་བཅོམ་ཚུལ་ཁྲིམས་རྗེས་སུ་བྱེད་པ་ཡི།
ཡན་ལག་བརྒྱད་པོ་འདི་དག་དང་ལྡན་ན།
གསོ་སྦྱོང་འདོད་སྤྱོད་ལྷ་ལུས་ཡིད་འོང་བ།
སྐྱེས་པ་བུད་མེད་དག་ལ་སྩོལ་བར་བགྱིད།། ༡༡ །།

སེར་སྣ་གཡོ་སྒྱུ་ཆགས་དང་སྙོམས་ལས་དང་།
མངོན་པའི་ང་རྒྱལ་འདོད་ཆགས་ཞེ་སྡང་དང་།
རིགས་དང་གཟུགས་དང་ཐོས་པ་ལང་ཚོ་དང་།
དབང་ཐང་ཆེ་བས་རྒྱགས་པ་དགྲ་བཞིན་གཟིགས། ༡༢།

བག་ཡོད་བདུད་རྩིའི་གནས་ཏེ་བག་མེད་པ།
འཆི་བའི་གནས་སུ་ཐུབ་པས་བཀའ་སྩལ་ཏེ།
དེ་བས་ཁྱོད་ཀྱི་དགེ་ཆོས་སྤེལ་སླད་དུ།
གུས་པས་རྟག་ཏུ་བག་དང་བཅས་པར་མཛོད། ༡༣།

གང་ཞིག་སྔོན་ཆད་བག་མེད་གྱུར་པ་ལགས།
ཕྱི་ནས་བག་དང་ལྡན་པར་གྱུར་དེ་ཡང་།
ཟླ་བ་སྤྲིན་བྲལ་ལྟ་བུར་རྣམ་མཛེས་ཏེ།
དགའ་བོ་སོར་ཕྲེང་མཐོང་ལྡན་བདེ་བྱེད་བཞིན། ༡༤།

འདི་ལྟར་བཟོད་མཚུངས་དཀའ་ཐུབ་མ་མཆིས་པས། །
ཁྱོད་ཀྱིས་ཁྲོ་བའི་གོ་སྐབས་དབྱེ་མི་བགྱི། །
ཁྲོ་བ་སྤངས་པས་ཕྱིར་མི་ལྡོག་པ་ཉིད། །
ཐོབ་པར་འགྱུར་བར་སངས་རྒྱས་ཞལ་གྱིས་བཞེས། ། ༡༥ ། །

བདག་ནི་འདིས་སྤྱོས་འདིས་བཏགས་ཕམ་པར་བྱས། །
འདི་ཡིས་བདག་ནོར་འཕྲོགས་པར་གྱུར་ཏོ་ཞེས། །
འཁོན་དུ་འཛིན་པས་འཁྲུག་ལོང་རྣམས་བསྐྱེད་དེ། །
འཁོན་འཛིན་རྣམས་སྤངས་བདེ་བར་གཉིད་ཀྱིས་ལོག ། ༡༦ ། །

སེམས་ནི་ཆུ་དང་ས་དང་རྡོ་བ་ལ། །
རི་མོ་བྲིས་པ་དེ་འདྲར་རིག་པར་བགྱི། །
དེའི་ནང་ཉོན་མོངས་ཅན་ལ་དང་པོ་ནི། །
མཆོག་སྟེ་ཆོས་འདོད་རྣམས་ལ་ཐ་མ་ལགས། ། ༡༧ ། །

ཀྱལ་བས་སྙིང་ལ་འཐབ་དང་བརྟེན་པ་དང་།
འོག་པར་སྨྲ་ལྡན་སྐྱེས་བུ་རྣམས་ཀྱི་ནི།
སྦྲང་རྩི་མེ་ཏོག་མི་གཙང་ལྟ་བུའི་ཚིག
རྣམ་གསུམ་བཀའ་སྩལ་དེ་ལས་ཐ་མ་སྤང་།། ༡༨།།

སྣང་ནས་སྣང་བའི་མཐར་ཐུག་མུན་པ་ནས།
མུན་པའི་མཐར་ཐུག་སྣང་ནས་མུན་མཐར་ཐུག།
མུན་ནས་སྣང་བའི་མཐར་ཐུག་གང་ཟག་ནི།
བཞི་སྟེ་དེ་དག་རྣམས་ཀྱི་དང་པོ་མཛོད།། ༡༩།།

མི་ནི་ཨ་མྲའི་འབྲས་བཞིན་མ་སྨིན་ལ།
སྨིན་པ་དང་འདྲ་སྨིན་ལ་མ་སྨིན་འདྲ།
མ་སྨིན་མ་སྨིན་པར་སྣང་སྨིན་ལ་ནི།
སྨིན་པར་སྣང་ཞེས་བགྱི་བར་འདུར་རྟོགས་མཛོད།། ༢༠།།

གཞན་གྱི་ཆུང་མ་མི་བལྟ་མཐོང་ན་ཡང་།

ན་ཚོད་མཐུན་པར་མ་དང་བུ་མོ་དང་།

སྲིང་མོའི་འདུ་ཤེས་བསྐྱེད་བགྱི་ཆགས་གྱུར་ན།

མི་གཙང་ཉིད་དུ་ཡང་དག་བསམ་པར་བགྱི།། ༣༡།།

གཡོ་བའི་སེམས་ནི་ཐོས་མཆོངས་བུ་ལྟ་བུར།

གཏེར་བཞིན་སྲོག་དང་འདྲ་བར་བསྲུང་བགྱི་སྟེ།

གདུག་པ་དུག་དང་མཚོན་དང་དགྲ་བོ་དང་།

མེ་བཞིན་འདོད་པའི་བདེ་ལ་ཡིད་འབྱུང་མཛོད།། ༣༢།།

འདོད་པ་རྣམས་ནི་ཕུང་བ་བསྐྱེད་པ་སྟེ།

རྒྱལ་བའི་དབང་པོས་ཀིམ་པའི་འབྲས་འདྲར་གསུངས།

དེ་དག་སྤང་བགྱི་དེ་ཡི་ལྕགས་སྒྲོག་གིས།

འཁོར་བའི་བཙོན་རར་འཇིག་རྟེན་འདི་དག་བཅིངས།། ༣༣།།

གང་དག་དབང་པོ་རྒྱུག་ཡུལ་རྣམས་ལ་ནི།
རྟག་ཏུ་མི་བརྟན་གཡོ་དང་གང་དག་ཅིག།
གཡུལ་ངོར་དགྲ་ཚོགས་ལས་རྒྱལ་དེ་དག་ལས།
མཁས་རྣམས་དང་པོ་དཔའ་རབ་ལགས་པར་འཚལ།། ༣༤

བུད་མེད་གཞོན་ནུའི་ལུས་ནི་ལོགས་ཤིག་ཏུ།
དྲི་ང་བ་དང་སྒོ་དགུ་ཛོད་པ་དང་།
མི་གཙང་ཀུན་སྣོད་འདྲ་བ་དགང་དཀའ་དང་།
པགས་པས་གཡོགས་པར་རྒྱན་ཡང་ལོགས་ཤིག་གཟིགས།། ༣༥

ཇི་ལྟར་མཛེ་ཅན་སྲིན་བུས་ཉེན་པ་ནི།
བདེ་བའི་དོན་དུ་མེ་ལ་ཀུན་བརྟེན་ཀྱང་།
ཞི་བར་མི་འགྱུར་དེ་དང་འདྲ་བར་ནི།
འདོད་པ་རྣམས་ལ་ཆགས་པའང་མཇུག་པར་མཛོད།། ༣༦

དོན་དམ་གཟིགས་པར་བགྱི་སྐྱོང་དངོས་རྣམས་ལ།
ཚུལ་བཞིན་ཡིད་ལ་བགྱིད་པ་དེ་བསྒོམས་མཛོད།
དེ་དང་འདྲ་བར་ཡོན་ཏན་ལྡན་པ་ཡི།
ཆོས་གཞན་འགའ་ཡང་མཆིས་པ་མ་ལགས་སོ།། ༣༥།།

སྐྱེས་བུ་རིགས་གཟུགས་ཐོས་དང་ལྡན་རྣམས་ཀྱང་།
ཤེས་དང་ཚུལ་ཁྲིམས་བྲལ་བ་བཀུར་མ་ལགས།
དེ་ལྟས་གང་ལ་ཡོན་ཏན་འདི་གཉིས་ལྡན།
དེ་ནི་ཡོན་ཏན་གཞན་དང་བྲལ་ཡང་མཆོད།། ༣༦།།

འཇིག་རྟེན་མཁྱེན་པ་རྙེད་དང་མི་རྙེད་དང་།
བདེ་དང་མི་བདེ་སྙན་དང་མི་སྙན་དང་།
བསྟོད་སྨད་ཅེས་བགྱི་འཇིག་རྟེན་ཆོས་བརྒྱད་པོ།
བདག་གི་ཡིད་ཡུལ་མིན་པར་མགོ་སྙོམས་མཛོད།། ༣༧།།

ཁྱོད་ཀྱིས་བྲམ་ཟེ་དགེ་སློང་ལྷ་དང་ནི།
མགྲོན་དང་ཡབ་ཡུམ་སྲས་དང་བཙུན་མོ་དང་།
འཁོར་གྱི་སླད་དུའང་སྡིག་པ་མི་བགྱི་སྟེ།
དམྱལ་བའི་རྣམ་སྨིན་སྐལ་ཆོད་འགའ་མ་མཆིས།། ༣༠།།

སྡིག་པའི་ལས་རྣམས་སྤྱད་པ་འགའ་ཡང་ནི།
དེ་ཡི་མོད་ལ་མཚོན་བཞིན་མི་གཅོད་ཀྱང་།
འཆི་བའི་དུས་ལ་བབ་ན་སྡིག་པ་ཡི།
ལས་ཀྱི་འབྲས་བུ་གང་ལགས་མངོན་པར་འགྱུར།། ༣༡།།

དད་དང་ཚུལ་ཁྲིམས་གཏོང་དང་ཐོས་པ་དང་།
དྲི་མེད་ངོ་ཚ་ཤེས་དང་ཁྲེལ་ཡོད་དང་།
ཤེས་རབ་ནོར་བདུན་ལགས་པར་ཐུབ་པས་གསུངས།
ནོར་གཞན་ཕལ་པ་དོན་མ་མཆིས་རྟོགས་མཛོད།། ༣༢།།

རྒྱན་པོ་འཕྱེད་དང་འདུས་ལ་བལྟ་བ་དང་།
ལེ་ལོ་སྡིག་པའི་གྲོགས་ལ་བརྟེན་པ་དང་།
ཆང་དང་མཚན་མོ་རྒྱུ་བ་ངན་སོང་བ།
གྲགས་པ་ཉམས་པར་འགྱུར་བ་དེ་དྲུག་སྤོང་།། ༣༣ །།

ནོར་རྣམས་ཀུན་གྱི་ནང་ནས་ཆོག་ཤེས་པ།
རབ་མཆོག་ལེགས་པར་ལྷ་མིའི་སྟོན་པས་གསུངས།
ཀུན་ཏུ་ཆོག་ཤེས་མཛོད་ཅིག་ཆོག་མཐུན་ན།
ནོར་མི་བདོག་ཀྱང་ཡང་དག་འབྱོར་པ་ལགས།། ༣༤ །།

ངེས་པ་བདོག་མང་ཇི་ལྟར་སྡུག་བསྔལ་བ།
འདོད་པ་ཆུང་རྣམས་དེ་ལྟ་མ་ལགས་ཏེ།
ཀླུ་མཆོག་རྣམས་ལ་མགོ་བོ་ཇི་སྙེད་པ།
དེ་ལས་བྱུང་བའི་སྡུག་བསྔལ་དེ་སྙེད་དོ།། ༣༥ །།

རང་བཞིན་དགྲར་འགྲེལ་གཤེད་མ་ལྟ་བུ་དང་།
ཁྱིམ་ཐབ་བརྙས་བྱེད་ཇོ་མོ་ལྟ་བུ་དང་།
ཆུང་དུའང་རྐུ་བ་ཆོམ་རྐུན་ལྟ་བུ་ཡི།
ཆུང་མ་གསུམ་པོ་དེ་དག་རྣམ་པར་སྤང་།། ༣༦ །།

སྲིང་མོ་ལྟ་བུར་རྗེས་མཐུན་གང་ཡིན་དང་།
མཛའ་མོ་བཞིན་དུ་སྙིང་ལ་འབབ་པ་དང་།
མ་བཞིན་ཕན་པར་འདོད་དང་བྲན་མོ་བཞིན།
དབང་གྱུར་གང་ཡིན་རིགས་ཀྱི་ལྷ་བཞིན་བཀུར།། ༣༧ །།

ཁ་ཟས་སྨན་དང་འདྲ་བར་རིགས་པ་ཡིས།
འདོད་ཆགས་ཞེ་སྡང་མེད་པར་བསྟེན་བགྱི་སྟེ།
རྒྱགས་ཕྱིར་མ་ལགས་བསྒྲིམས་པའི་ཕྱིར་མ་ལགས།
མཆོག་ཕྱིར་མ་ལགས་ལུས་གནས་འབའ་ཞིག་ཕྱིར། ༣༨ །།

རིགས་པའི་བདག་ཉིད་ཉིན་པར་མཐའ་དག་དང་།
མཚན་མོའི་ཐུན་གྱི་སྟོད་སྨད་འདས་ན་ནི།
མནལ་ཚེའང་འབྲས་བུ་མེད་པར་མི་འགྱུར་བར།
དྲན་དང་ལྡན་པར་དེ་དག་བར་དུ་མནོལ།། ༣༩ ||

བྱམས་དང་སྙིང་རྗེ་དག་དང་དགའ་བ་དང་།
བཏང་སྙོམས་རྟག་ཏུ་ཡང་དག་བསྒོམས་པར་བགྱི།
གོང་མ་བརྙེད་པར་མ་གྱུར་དེ་ལྟ་ནའང་།
ཚངས་པའི་འཇིག་རྟེན་བདེ་བ་ཐོབ་པར་འགྱུར།། ༤༠ ||

འདོད་སྤྱོད་དགའ་དང་བདེ་དང་སྡུག་བསྔལ་དག།
རྣམ་པར་སྤངས་པའི་བསམ་གཏན་བཞི་པོ་ཡིས།
ཚངས་དང་འོད་གསལ་དག་དང་དགེ་རྒྱས་དང་།
འབྲས་བུ་ཆེ་ལྡན་རྣམས་དང་སྐལ་མཉམ་ཐོབ།། ༤༡ ||

རྟག་དང་མངོན་པར་ཞེན་དང་གཉེན་པོ་མེད། །
ཡོན་ཏན་གཙོ་ལྡན་གཞི་ལས་བྱུང་བའི་ལས། །
དགེ་དང་མི་དགེ་རྣམ་ལྔ་ཆེན་པོ་སྟེ། །
དེ་ལས་དགེ་བ་སྤྱོད་ལ་བརྩོན་པར་བགྱི། ། ༤༢།།

ལན་ཚ་སྲང་འགས་ཆུ་ནི་ཉུང་དུ་ཞིག །
རོ་སྒྱུར་བགྱིད་ཀྱི་གངྒའི་ཀླུང་མིན་ལྟར། །
དེ་བཞིན་སྡིག་པའི་ལས་ནི་ཆུང་དུ་ཡང་། །
དགེ་བའི་རྩ་བ་ཡངས་ལ་མཁྱེན་པར་མཛོད། ། ༤༣།།

རྒོད་དང་འགྱོད་དང་གནོད་སེམས་རྨུགས་པ་དང་། །
གཉིད་དང་འདོད་ལ་འདུན་དང་ཐེ་ཚོམ་སྟེ། །
སྒྲིབ་པ་ལྔ་པོ་འདི་དག་དགེ་བའི་ནོར། །
འཕྲོག་པའི་ཆོམ་རྐུན་ལགས་པར་མཁྱེན་པར་མཛོད། ། ༤༤།།

དད་དང་བརྩོན་འགྲུས་དག་དང་དྲན་པ་དང་།
ཏིང་འཛིན་ཤེས་རབ་ཆོས་མཆོག་ལྔ་ཉིད་དེ།
འདི་ལ་མངོན་བརྩོན་མཛོད་ཅིག་འདི་དག་ནི།
སྟོབས་དབང་ཞེས་བགྱི་རྩེ་མོར་གྱུར་པའང་ལགས།། ༤༥།།

ན་རྒ་འཆི་སྡུག་བྲལ་དང་དེ་བཞིན་དུ།
ལས་ནི་བདག་གིར་བྱ་ལས་མ་འདས་ཞེས།
དེ་ལྟར་ཡང་དང་ཡང་དུ་སེམས་པ་ནི།
དེ་ཡི་གཉེན་པོའི་སྒོ་ནས་རྒྱགས་མི་འགྱུར།། ༤༦།།

གལ་ཏེ་མཐོ་རིས་ཐར་པ་མངོན་བཞེད་ན།
ཡང་དག་ལྟ་ལ་གོམས་པ་ཉིད་དུ་མཛོད།
གང་ཟག་ལོག་པར་ལྟ་བས་ལེགས་སྤྱད་ཀྱང་།
ཐམས་ཅད་རྣམ་པར་སྨིན་པ་མི་བཟད་ལྡན།། ༤༧།།

མི་ནི་ཡང་དག་ཉིད་དུ་མི་བདེ་ཞིང་།
མི་རྟག་བདག་མེད་མི་གཙང་རིག་པར་བགྱི།
དྲན་པ་ཉེ་བར་མ་གཞག་རྣམས་ཀྱིས་ནི།
ཕྱིན་ཅི་ལོག་བཞིར་ལྟ་བ་ཕུང་བྲོལ་བ།། ༤༨།།

གཟུགས་ནི་བདག་མ་ཡིན་ཞེས་གསུངས་ཏེ་བདག།
གཟུགས་དང་ལྡན་མིན་གཟུགས་ལ་བདག་གནས་མིན།
བདག་ལ་གཟུགས་མི་གནས་ཏེ་དེ་བཞིན་དུ།
ཕུང་པོ་ལྷག་མ་བཞི་ཡང་སྟོང་རྟོགས་བགྱི།། ༤༩།།

ཕུང་པོ་འདོད་རྒྱལ་ལས་མིན་དུས་ལས་མིན།
རང་བཞིན་ལས་མིན་ངོ་བོ་ཉིད་ལས་མིན།
དབང་ཕྱུག་ལས་མིན་རྒྱུ་མེད་ཅན་མིན་ཏེ།
མི་ཤེས་ལས་དང་སྲེད་ལས་བྱུང་རིག་མཛོད།། ༥༠།།

ཚུལ་ཁྲིམས་བརྟུལ་ཞུགས་མཆོག་འཛིན་རང་ལུས་ལ།
ཕྱིན་ཅི་ལོག་པར་ལྟ་དང་ཐེ་ཚོམ་སྟེ།
ཀུན་ཏུ་སྦྱོར་བ་འདི་གསུམ་ཐར་པ་ཡི།
གྲོང་ཁྱེར་སྒོ་འགེགས་ལགས་པར་མཁྱེན་པར་མཛོད།། ༥༡།།

ཐར་པ་བདག་ལ་རག་ལས་འདི་ལ་ནི།
གཞན་གྱིས་གྲོགས་བགྱིད་ཅི་ཡང་མ་མཆིས་པས།
ཐོས་དང་ཚུལ་ཁྲིམས་བསམ་གཏན་ལྡན་པ་ཡིས།
བདེན་པ་རྣམ་པ་བཞི་ལ་འབད་པར་མཛོད།། ༥༢།།

ལྷག་པའི་ཚུལ་ཁྲིམས་ལྷག་པའི་ཤེས་རབ་དང་།
ལྷག་པའི་སེམས་ལ་རྟག་ཏུ་བསླབ་པར་བགྱི།
བསླབ་པ་བརྒྱ་རྩ་ལྔ་བཅུ་ལྷག་གཅིག་ནི།
གསུམ་པོ་འདི་ནང་ཡང་དག་འདུ་བར་འགྱུར།། ༥༣།།

དབང་ཕྱུག་ལུས་རྟོགས་དྲན་པ་བདེར་གཤེགས་ཀྱིས།
བགྲོད་པ་གཅིག་པའི་ལམ་དུ་ཉེ་བར་བསྟན།
དེ་ནི་བསྒྲིམས་ནས་མངོན་པར་བསྲུང་བགྱི་སྟེ།
དྲན་པ་ཉམས་པས་ཆོས་རྣམས་འཇིག་པར་འགྱུར།། ༥༤།།

ཚེ་ནི་གནོད་མང་རླུང་གིས་བཏབ་པ་ཡི།
ཆུ་ཡི་ཆུ་བུར་བས་ཀྱང་མི་རྟག་ན།
དབུགས་རྔུབ་དབུགས་འབྱུང་གཉིད་ཀྱིས་ལོག་པ་ལས།
སད་ཁོམ་གང་ལགས་དེ་ནི་ངོ་མཚར་ཆེ།། ༥༥།།

ལུས་མཐའ་ཐལ་བ་མཐར་སྐམ་མཐར་འདྲུལ་ཞིང་།
ཐ་མར་མི་གཙང་སྙིང་པོ་མ་མཆིས་པར།
རྣམ་པར་འཇིག་ངེས་ཞུགས་པར་འགྱུར་བ་སྟེ།
སོ་སོར་འཇིག་ཆོས་ཅན་དུ་མཁྱེན་པར་མཛོད།། ༥༦།།

ས་དང་ལྷུན་པོ་རྒྱ་མཚོ་ཉི་མ་བདུན། །
འབར་བས་བསྲེགས་པས་ལུས་ཅན་འདི་དག་ཀྱང་། །
ཐལ་བ་ཙམ་ཡང་ལུས་པར་མི་འགྱུར་ན། །
ཤིན་ཏུ་ཉམ་ཆུང་མི་ལྟ་སྨོས་ཅི་འཚལ།། ༥༧།།

དེ་ལྟར་འདི་ཀུན་མི་རྟག་བདག་མེད་དེ། །
སྐྱབས་མེད་མགོན་མེད་གནས་མེད་དེ་སྐྱོད་དུ། །
འཁོར་བ་ཆུ་ཤིང་སྙིང་པོ་མེད་པ་ལ། །
མི་མཆོག་ཁྱོད་ཀྱིས་ཐུགས་ནི་འབྱུང་བར་མཛོད།། ༥༨།།

རྒྱ་མཚོ་གཅིག་གནས་གཉའ་ཤིང་བུ་ག་དང་། །
རུས་སྦལ་ཕྲད་པ་བས་ཀྱང་དུད་འགྲོ་ལས། །
མི་ཉིད་ཆེས་ཐོབ་དཀའ་བས་མི་དབང་གིས། །
དམ་ཆོས་སྤྱད་པས་དེ་འབྲས་མཆིས་པར་མཛོད།། ༥༩།།

གང་ཞིག་གསེར་སྣོད་རིན་ཆེན་སྤྲས་པ་ཡིས།
ངན་སྐྱུགས་འཕྱག་པར་བགྱིད་པ་དེ་བས་ཀྱང་།
གང་ཞིག་མི་རུ་སྐྱེས་ནས་སྡིག་པ་དག
བགྱིད་པ་དེ་ནི་ཆེས་རབ་བླུན་པ་ལགས།། ༨༠ ༎

མཐུན་པར་གྱུར་པའི་ཡུལ་ན་གནས་པ་དང་།
སྐྱེས་བུ་དམ་པ་ལ་ནི་བརྟེན་པ་དང་།
བདག་ཉིད་ལེགས་སྨོན་སྔོན་ཡང་བསོད་ནམས་བགྱིས།
འཁོར་ལོ་ཆེན་པོ་བཞི་ནི་ཁྱོད་ལ་མངའ།། ༨༡ ༎

དགེ་བའི་བཤེས་གཉེན་བརྟེན་པ་ཚངས་པར་སྤྱོད།
ཡོངས་སུ་རྫོགས་པར་ཐུབ་པས་གསུངས་དེའི་ཕྱིར།
སྐྱེས་བུ་དམ་པ་བརྟེན་འགྲོ་རྒྱལ་བ་ལ།
བརྟེན་ནས་རབ་ཏུ་མང་པོས་ཞི་བ་ཐོབ།། ༨༢ ༎

ལོག་པར་ལྟ་བ་འཛིན་དང་དུད་འགྲོ་དང་།
ཡི་དྭགས་ཉིད་དང་དམྱལ་བར་སྐྱེ་བ་དང་།
རྒྱལ་བའི་བཀའ་མེད་པ་དང་མཐའ་འཁོབ་ཏུ།
ཀླ་ཀློར་སྐྱེ་དང་གླེན་ཞིང་ལྐུགས་པ་ཉིད།། ༦༣།།

ཚེ་རིང་ལྷ་དང་གང་ཡང་རུང་བར་ནི།
སྐྱེ་བ་ཞེས་བགྱི་མི་ཁོམ་སྐྱོན་བརྒྱད་པོ།
དེ་དག་དང་བྲལ་ཁོམ་པ་རྙེད་ནས་ནི།
སྐྱེ་བ་བཟློག་པའི་སླད་དུ་འབད་པར་མཛོད།། ༦༤།།

རེས་པ་འདོད་པས་ཕོངས་དང་འཆི་བ་དང་།
ན་དང་རྒ་སོགས་སྡུག་བསྔལ་དུ་མ་ཡིས།
འབྱུང་གནས་འཁོར་བ་ལ་ནི་སྐྱོ་མཛོད་ཅིང་།
འདི་ཡི་ཉེས་པ་ཕལ་ཀྱང་གསན་པར་མཛོད།། ༦༥།།

ཕ་ནི་བུ་ཉིད་མ་ནི་ཆུང་མ་ཉིད།
སྐྱེ་བོ་དགྲ་གྱུར་པ་དག་བཤེས་ཉིད་དང་།
བཟློག་པ་ཉིད་དུ་མཆི་བས་དེ་སྐད་དུ།
འཁོར་བ་དག་ན་ངེས་པ་འགའ་མ་མཆིས།། ༦༦།།

རེ་རེས་རྒྱ་མཚོ་བཞི་ལས་ལྷག་པ་ཡི།
འོ་མ་འཐུངས་ཏེ་ད་དུང་སོ་སོ་ཡི།
སྐྱེ་བོའི་རྗེས་སུ་འབྲང་བའི་འཁོར་བ་པས།
དེ་བས་ཆེས་མང་ཉིད་ཅིག་བཏུང་འཚལ་ལོ།། ༦༧།།

རེ་རེས་བདག་ཉིད་རུས་པའི་ཕུང་པོ་ནི།
ལྷུན་པོ་མཉམ་པ་སྐྱེད་ཅིག་འདས་གྱུར་ཏེ།
ས་ཡི་ཐུག་མཐའ་རྒྱ་ཤུག་ཚིག་གུ་ཙམ།
རིལ་བུར་བགྲངས་ཀྱང་མ་ཡིས་ལང་མི་འགྱུར།། ༦༨།།

བརྒྱ་བྱིན་འཇིག་རྟེན་མཆོད་འོས་གྱུར་ནས་ནི།
ལས་ཀྱི་དབང་གིས་ཕྱིར་ཡང་ས་སྟེང་ལྷུང་།
འཁོར་ལོས་བསྒྱུར་རྒྱལ་ཉིད་དུ་གྱུར་ནས་ཀྱང་།
འཁོར་བ་དག་ཏུ་ཡང་བྲན་ཉིད་དུ་འགྱུར།། ༨༩།།

མཐོ་རིས་བུ་མོའི་ནུ་མ་སྣེད་པ་ལ།
རེག་པའི་བདེ་བ་ཡུན་རིང་སྤྱོད་ནས་སླར།
དམྱལ་བར་འཐག་གཅོད་དབང་བའི་འབྲུལ་འཁོར་གྱི།
རེག་པ་ཤིན་ཏུ་མི་བཟད་བསྙེན་འཚལ་ལོ།། ༩༠།།

རྐང་པའི་རེག་པས་ཉམས་པར་བདེ་བཟོད་པ།
ལྷུན་པོའི་སྒོ་ལ་ཡུན་རིང་གནས་ནས་ནི།
སླར་ཡང་མེ་མུར་རོ་མྱགས་རྒྱུ་བ་ཡི།
སྡུག་བསྔལ་མི་བཟད་འཕོག་སྙམ་བགྱིད་འཚལ་ལོ།། ༩༡།།

མཐོ་རིས་བུ་མོས་འགྲོངས་ཞིང་དགའ་བ་དང་།
རྣམ་པར་མཛེས་ཚལ་སོན་པར་རྩེས་ནས་སླར།
འདབ་མ་རལ་གྲི་འདྲ་ཚལ་གནས་རྣམས་ཀྱིས།
རྐང་ལག་རྣ་བ་སྣ་གཅོད་འཐོབ་པར་འགྱུར།། ༥༢།།

དལ་གྱིས་འབབ་པར་ལྷ་ཡི་བུ་མོ་ནི།
གཞོང་མཛེས་གསེར་གྱི་པདྨར་ལྡན་ཞུགས་ནས།
སླར་ཡང་དམྱལ་བར་ཆུ་བོ་རབ་མེད་པ།
ཚ་སྒོ་བཟོད་གླགས་ཆུ་ཆེན་འཇུག་འཚལ་ལོ།། ༥༣།།

ལྷ་ཡུལ་འདོད་བདེ་ཤིན་ཏུ་ཆེན་པོ་དང་།
ཚངས་ཉིད་ཆགས་བྲལ་བདེ་བ་ཐོབ་ནས་སླར།
མནར་མེད་མེ་ཡི་བུད་ཤིང་གྱུར་པ་ཡི།
སྡུག་བསྔལ་རྒྱུན་མི་འཆད་པ་བསྙེན་འཚལ་ལོ།། ༥༤།།

ཉི་མ་ཟླ་བ་ཉིད་ཐོབ་རང་ལུས་ཀྱི།
འོད་ཀྱིས་འཇིག་རྟེན་མཐའ་དག་སྣང་བྱས་ཏེ།
སླར་ཡང་མུན་ནག་སྨག་ཏུ་ཕྱིན་གྱུར་ནས།
རང་གི་ལག་པ་བརྐྱངས་པའང་མི་མཐོང་འགྱུར།། ༩༥།།

དེ་ལྟར་ཟོངས་པར་འགྱུར་འཚལ་བསོད་ནམས་ནི།
རྣམ་གསུམ་མར་མེའི་སྣང་བ་རབ་བཞེས་ཤིག།
གཅིག་པུ་ཉི་མ་ཟླ་བས་མི་བརྡེ་བའི།
མུན་ནག་མཐའ་ཡས་ནང་དུ་འཇུག་འཚལ་ལོ།། ༩༦།།

སེམས་ཅན་ཉེས་པ་སྤྱད་པ་སྤྱོད་རྣམས་ལ།
ཡང་སོས་ཐིག་ནག་རབ་ཏུ་ཚ་བ་དང་།
བསྡུས་འཛོམས་ངུ་འབོད་མནར་མེད་ལ་སོགས་པའི།
དམྱལ་བ་རྣམས་སུ་རྟག་ཏུ་སྡུག་བསྔལ་འགྱུར།། ༩༧།།

ཁ་ཅིག་ཉི་ལ་བཞིན་འཚེར་ཏེ་དེ་བཞིན་གཞན།
ཕྱི་མ་ཞིབ་མོ་བཞིན་དུ་ཕྱི་མར་རྙོག།
ཁ་ཅིག་སོག་ལེ་དྲ་སྐྱེ་དེ་བཞིན་གཞན།
སྐྱ་རེ་མི་བཟད་སོ་རྣོན་རྣམས་ཀྱིས་གཤེག། ༨༨།།

དེ་བཞིན་གཞན་དག་ཁྲོ་རྒྱུ་ཞུགས་པ་ཡི།
ཁུ་བ་འབར་བ་འཁྲིགས་པ་ལྷུང་བར་བགྱིད།
ཁ་ཅིག་ལྕགས་ཀྱི་གསལ་ཤིང་མེ་འབར་བ།
ཚེར་མ་ཅན་ལ་ཀུན་ཏུ་བརྒྱུད་པར་བགྱིད།། ༨༩།།

ཁ་ཅིག་ལྕགས་ཀྱི་མཆེ་བ་ལྡན་པའི་ཁྱི།
གཏུམ་པོས་དཔང་ཅིང་ལག་པ་གནམ་དུ་བསྒྲེང་།
དབང་མེད་གཞན་དག་ལྕགས་མཆུ་རྣོན་པོ་དང་།
སེན་མོ་མི་བཟད་ལྡན་པའི་ཁ་རྣམས་འཐོག། ༩༠།།

ཁ་ཅིག་སྲིན་བུ་སྦུར་པ་ལྟ་ཚོགས་དང་།
ཀ་སྐྱང་སྐྱུང་མ་ནག་པོ་བྲེ་ཁྲག་དག།
རིག་ན་མི་བཟད་རྨ་སྦྲུལ་ཆེར་འབྱིན་པས།
ཟ་བར་བགྱིད་ཅིང་འདྲེ་ཕྱོག་སྐྱེ་སྦྲགས་འདོན།། ༨༧།།

ཁ་ཅིག་མདག་མ་འབར་བའི་ཚོགས་སུ་ནི།
རྒྱུན་མི་ཆད་པར་རབ་བསྒྲེགས་ཁ་ཡང་བགྲད།
ཁ་ཅིག་ལྕགས་ལས་བྲུས་པའི་ཟངས་ཆེན་དུ།
སྤྱིའུ་ཚུགས་འབྲས་ཀྱི་ཐུག་པ་བཞིན་དུ་འཚོད།། ༨༨།།

སྡིག་ཅན་དབུགས་འབྱུང་འགག་པ་ཙམ་ཞིག་གི།
དུས་ཀྱི་བར་དུ་ཆོད་ཉམས་དགྱལ་བ་ཡི།
སྡུག་བསྔལ་གཞལ་ཡས་ཐོས་ནས་རྣམ་སྟོང་དུ།
མི་འཇིགས་གང་ལགས་རྡོ་རྗེའི་རང་བཞིན་ནོ།། ༨༩།།

དམྱལ་བ་བྲིས་པ་མཐོང་དང་ཐོས་པ་དང་།
དྲན་དང་བཀླགས་དང་གཟུགས་སུ་བགྱིས་རྣམས་ཀྱང་།
འཇིགས་པ་བསྐྱེད་པར་འགྱུར་ན་མི་བཟད་པའི།
རྣམ་སྨིན་ཉམས་སུ་མྱོང་ན་སྨོས་ཅི་འཚལ།། ༨༤ ||

བདེ་བ་ཀུན་གྱི་ནང་ན་སྲེད་ཟད་པའི།
བདེ་བའི་བདག་པོ་བགྱིད་པ་ཇི་ལྟ་བར།
དེ་བཞིན་སྡུག་བསྔལ་ཀུན་གྱི་ནང་ན་ནི།
མནར་མེད་དམྱལ་བའི་སྡུག་བསྔལ་རབ་མི་བཟད།། ༨༥ ||

འདི་ན་ཉིན་གཅིག་མདུང་ཐུང་སུམ་བརྒྱ་ཡིས།
རབ་ཏུ་དྲག་བཏབ་སྡུག་བསྔལ་གང་ལགས་པ།
དེས་ནི་དམྱལ་བའི་སྡུག་བསྔལ་ཆུང་ངུ་ལའང་།
འོལ་ཡང་མི་བགྲི་ཆར་ཡང་མི་ཕོད་དོ།། ༨༦ ||

དེ་ལྟར་སྡུག་བསྔལ་ཤིན་ཏུ་མི་བཟད་པོ།
བྱེ་བ་ཕྲག་བརྒྱར་ཉམས་སུ་མྱོང་ཡང་ནི།
ཇི་སྲིད་མི་དགེ་དེ་ཟད་མ་གྱུར་པ།
དེ་སྲིད་སྲོག་དང་བྲལ་བར་མི་འགྱུར་རོ།། ༨༧ ||

མི་དགེའི་འབྲས་འདི་རྣམས་ཀྱི་ས་བོན་ནི།
ལུས་ངག་ཡིད་ཀྱི་ཉེས་སྤྱོད་ཕྱོད་ཀྱིས་ནི།
ཅི་ནས་དེ་རྡུལ་ཙམ་ཡང་མ་མཆིས་པ།
དེ་ལྟར་ཉིད་ཀྱི་རྩོལ་གྱིས་འབད་པར་མཛོད།། ༨༨ ||

དུད་འགྲོའི་སྐྱེ་གནས་ན་ཡང་གསོད་པ་དང་།
བཅིང་དང་བརྡེག་སོགས་སྡུག་བསྔལ་སྣ་ཚོགས་པ།
ཞི་འགྱུར་དགེ་བ་སྤངས་པ་རྣམས་ལ་ནི།
གཅིག་ལ་གཅིག་ཟ་ཤིན་ཏུ་མི་བཟད་པ།། ༨༩ ||

ཁ་ཅིག་མུ་ཏིག་བལ་དང་རུས་པ་དང་།
ཤ་དང་པགས་པའི་ཆེད་དུ་འཆི་བར་འགྱུར།
དབང་མེད་གཞན་དག་རྡོག་པ་ལག་པ་དང་།
ལྕག་དང་ལྕགས་ཀྱུ་གདབ་ཅས་བཏབ་སྟེ་བཀོལ།། ༨༠།།

ཡི་དྭགས་ན་ཡང་འདོད་པས་ཕོངས་པ་ཡིས།
བསྐྱེད་པའི་སྡུག་བསྔལ་རྒྱུན་ཆགས་མི་འཚོས་པ།
བཀྲེས་སྐོམ་གྲང་དྲོ་ངལ་དང་འཇིགས་པ་ཡིས།
བསྐྱེད་པ་ཤིན་ཏུ་མི་བཟད་བསྟེན་འཚལ་ལོ།། ༨༡།།

ཁ་ཅིག་ཁ་ནི་ཁབ་ཀྱི་མིག་ཙམ་ལ།
ལྟོ་བ་རི་ཡི་གཏོས་ཙམ་བཀྲེས་པས་ཉེན།
མི་གཙང་ཕྱི་ནར་བོར་བ་ཅུང་ཟད་ཀྱང་།
འཚོལ་བའི་མཐུ་དང་ལྡན་པ་མ་ལགས་སོ།། ༨༢།།

ཁ་ཅིག་པགས་རུས་ལུས་ཤིང་གཅེར་བུ་སྐྱེ།
ཏ་ལ་ཡ་ཐོག་བསྐམས་པ་ལྟ་བུ་ལགས།
ཁ་ཅིག་མཚན་ཞིང་ཁ་ནས་འབར་བ་སྐྱེ།
ཟས་སུ་འབར་བའི་ཁ་བབས་ཐེ་མ་འཚལ།། ༨༣།།

སྐྱད་རིགས་འགས་ནི་ཟུག་དང་ཕྱེ་ས་དང་།
ཁྲག་སོགས་མི་གཙང་བ་ཡང་མི་རྙེད་དེ།
ཕན་ཚུན་གདོང་དུ་འཚོག་ཅིང་མགྲིན་པ་ནས།
འབྲུ་བ་རྫུང་བ་སྨིན་པའི་ཟུག་འཚལ་ལོ།། ༨༤།།

འདི་དག་རྣམས་ལ་སོ་གའི་དུས་སུ་ནི།
ཟླ་བའང་ཚ་ལ་དགུན་ནི་ཉི་མའང་གྲང་།
ལྗོན་ཤིང་འབྲས་བུ་མེད་འགྱུར་འདི་དག་གིས།
བལྟས་པ་ཙམ་གྱིས་ཀླུང་ཡང་བསྐམས་པར་འགྱུར།། ༨༥།།

བར་ཆད་མེད་པར་སྡུག་བསྔལ་བསྟེན་གྱུར་པ།
ཉེས་པར་སྤྱོད་པའི་ལས་ཀྱི་ཞགས་པ་ནི།
སྲ་བས་བཅིངས་པའི་ལུས་ཅན་ཁ་ཅིག་ལོ།
ལྔ་སྟོང་དག་དང་ཁྲི་ཡང་འཆིར་མི་འགྱུར།། ༩༦ །།

དེ་ལྟར་ཡི་དྭགས་རྣམས་ཀྱིས་སྣ་ཚོགས་པའི།
སྡུག་བསྔལ་རོ་གཅིག་ཐོབ་པ་གང་ལགས་པ།
དེ་ཡི་རྒྱུ་ནི་སྐྱེ་བོ་འཛུངས་དགའ་བ།
སེར་སྣ་འཕགས་མིན་ལགས་པར་སངས་རྒྱས་གསུངས།། ༩༧

མཐོ་རིས་ན་ཡང་བདེ་ཆེན་དེ་དག་གི།
འཆི་འཕོའི་སྡུག་བསྔལ་ཉིད་ནི་དེ་བས་ཆེ།
དེ་ལྟར་བསམ་ནས་ཡ་རབས་རྣམས་ཀྱིས་ནི།
ཟད་འགྱུར་མཐོ་རིས་སླད་དུ་སྲིད་མི་བགྱི།། ༩༨ །།

ལུས་ཀྱི་ཁ་དོག་མི་སྡུག་འགྱུར་བ་དང་།
སྟན་ལ་མི་དགའ་མེ་ཏོག་ཕྲེང་རྙིངས་དང་།
གོས་ལ་དྲི་མ་ཆགས་དང་ལུས་ལ་ནི།
སྔོན་ཆད་མེད་པའི་རྔུལ་འབྱུང་ཞེས་བགྱི་བ།། ༩༩ ༎

མཐོ་རིས་འཆི་འཕོ་སྨྲོན་བྱེད་ལྟ་ལྟས་ལྔ།
མཐོ་རིས་གནས་པའི་ལྷ་རྣམས་ལ་འབྱུང་སྟེ།
ས་སྟེང་མི་རྣམས་འཆི་བར་འགྱུར་བ་དག
སྨྲོན་པར་བྱེད་པའི་འཆི་ལྟས་རྣམས་དང་འདྲ།། ༡༠༠ ༎

ལྷ་ཡི་འཇིག་རྟེན་དག་ནས་འཕོས་པ་ལ།
གལ་ཏེ་དགེ་བའི་ལྷག་མ་འགའ་མེད་ན།
དེ་ནས་དབང་མེད་དུད་འགྲོ་ཡི་དྭགས་དང་།
དམྱལ་བར་གནས་པ་གང་ཡང་རུང་བར་འགྱུར།། ༡༠༡ ༎

ལྷ་མིན་དག་ནའང་རང་བཞིན་གྱིས་ལྷ་ཡི།
དཔལ་ལ་སྡང་ཕྱིར་ཡིད་ཀྱི་སྡུག་བསྔལ་ཆེ།
དེ་དག་བློ་དང་ལྡན་ནའང་འགྲོ་བ་ཡི།
སྒྲིབ་པས་བདེན་པ་མཐོང་བ་མ་མཆིས་སོ།། ༡༠༢།།

འཁོར་བ་དེ་འདྲ་ལགས་པས་ལྷ་མི་དང་།
དམྱལ་བ་ཡི་དྭགས་དུད་འགྲོ་རྣམས་དག་ཏུ།
སྐྱེ་བ་བཟང་པོ་མ་ལགས་སྐྱེ་བ་ནི།
གནོད་པ་དུ་མའི་སྣོད་གྱུར་ལགས་མཁྱེན་མཛོད།། ༡༠༣།།

མགོའམ་གོས་ལ་གློ་བུར་མེ་འབར་ན།
དེ་དག་ཕྱིར་བཟློག་བགྱི་བ་བཏང་ནས་ཀྱང་།
ཡང་སྲིད་མེད་པར་བགྱི་སླད་འབད་འཚལ་ཏེ།
དེ་བས་ཆེས་མཆོག་དགོས་པ་གཞན་མ་མཆིས།། ༡༠༤།།

ཚུལ་ཁྲིམས་དག་དང་ཤེས་རབ་བསམ་གཏན་གྱིས།
མྱ་ངན་འདས་ཞི་དུལ་བ་དྲི་མེད་པའི།
གོ་འཕང་མི་རྒ་མི་འཆི་ཟད་མི་འཚེལ།
ས་ཆུ་མེ་རླུང་ཉི་ཟླ་བྲལ་ཐོབ་མཛོད།། ༡༠༥ །།

དྲན་དང་ཆོས་རབ་འབྱེད་དང་བརྩོན་འགྲུས་དང་།
དགའ་དང་ཤིན་ཏུ་སྦྱངས་དང་ཏིང་འཛིན་དང་།
བཏང་སྙོམས་འདི་བདུན་བྱང་ཆུབ་ཡན་ལག་སྟེ།
མྱ་ངན་འདས་ཐོབ་བྱེད་པའི་དགེ་ཚོགས་ལགས།། ༡༠༦ །།

ཤེས་རབ་མེད་པར་བསམ་གཏན་ཡོད་མིན་ཏེ།
བསམ་གཏན་མེད་པར་ཡང་ནི་ཤེས་རབ་མེད།
གང་ལ་དེ་གཉིས་ཡོད་པས་སྲིད་པ་ཡི།
རྒྱ་མཚོ་གནག་རྗེས་ལྟ་བུར་འཚལ་བར་བགྱི།། ༡༠༧ །།

ལུང་མ་བསྟན་པ་བཅུ་བཞི་འཇིག་རྟེན་ན།
ཉི་མའི་གཉེན་གྱིས་རབ་གསུངས་གང་ལགས་པ།
དེ་དག་རྣམས་ལ་བསམ་པར་མི་བགྱི་སྟེ།
དེ་ཡིས་བློ་ནི་ཞི་བར་བགྱིད་མ་ལགས།། ༡༠༨ ༎

མ་རིག་པ་ལས་ལས་ཏེ་དེ་ལས་ནི།
རྣམ་ཤེས་དེ་ལས་མིང་དང་གཟུགས་རབ་འབྱུང་།
དེ་ལས་སྐྱེ་མཆེད་དྲུག་སྟེ་དེ་ལས་ནི།
རེག་པ་ཀུན་ཏུ་འབྱུང་བར་ཐུབ་པས་གསུངས།། ༡༠༩ ༎

རེག་པ་ལས་ནི་ཚོར་བ་ཀུན་འབྱུང་སྟེ།
ཚོར་བའི་གཞི་ལས་སྲེད་པ་འབྱུང་བར་འགྱུར།
སྲེད་ལས་ལེན་པ་སྐྱེ་བར་འགྱུར་བ་སྟེ།
དེ་ལས་སྲིད་པ་སྲིད་ལས་སྐྱེ་བ་ལགས།། ༡༡༠ ༎

སྐྱེ་བ་ཡོད་ན་མྱ་ངན་ན་ན་རྒ་དང་།
འདོད་པས་ཕོངས་དང་འཆི་བས་འཇིགས་སོགས་ཀྱི།
སྡུག་བསྔལ་ཕུང་པོ་ཀུན་ཏུ་ཆེ་འབྱུང་སྟེ།
སྐྱེ་བ་འགག་པས་འདི་ཀུན་འགག་པར་འགྱུར།། ༡༡༡།།

རྟེན་ཅིང་འབྲེལ་བར་འབྱུང་འདི་རྒྱལ་བ་ཡི།
གསུང་གི་མཛོད་ཀྱི་གཅེས་པ་ཟབ་མོ་སྟེ།
གང་གིས་འདི་ནི་ཡང་དག་མཐོང་བ་དེས།
སངས་རྒྱས་དེ་ཉིད་རིག་པ་རྣམ་མཆོག་མཐོང་།། ༡༡༢།།

ཡང་དག་ལྟ་དང་འཚོ་དང་རྩོལ་བ་དང་།
དྲན་དང་ཏིང་འཛིན་ངག་དང་ལས་མཐའ་དང་།
ཡང་དག་རྟོག་ཉིད་ལམ་གྱི་ཡན་ལག་བརྒྱད།
འདི་ནི་ཞི་བར་བགྱི་སླད་བསྒོམ་པར་བགྱི།། ༡༡༣།།

སྐྱེ་འདི་སྡུག་བསྔལ་སྐྱེད་པ་ཞེས་བགྱི་བ།
དེ་ནི་དེ་ཡི་ཀུན་འབྱུང་རྒྱ་ཆེན་ཏེ།
འདི་འགོག་པ་ནི་ཐར་པ་ལགས་ཏེ་ལམ།
དེ་ཐོབ་འཕགས་ལམ་ཡན་ལག་བརྒྱད་ལགས།། ༡༡༤།།

དེ་ལྟར་ལགས་པས་འཕགས་པའི་བདེན་པ་བཞི།
མཐོང་བར་བགྱི་སླད་རྟག་ཏུ་བརྩོན་པར་བགྱི།
ཡང་ན་དཔལ་ལ་གནས་ཁྱིམ་པ་རྣམས་ཀྱིས་ཀྱང་།
ཤེས་པས་ཉོན་མོངས་ཆུ་བོ་ལས་བརྒལ་བགྱི།། ༡༡༥།།

གང་དག་ཆོས་མངོན་འབྲེལ་པ་དེ་དག་ཀྱང་།
གནམ་ལས་བབས་པ་མ་ལགས་ལོ་ཐོག་བཞིན།
ས་རུམ་ནས་འཐོན་མ་ལགས་དེ་དག་སྔོན།
ཉོན་མོངས་རག་ལས་སྐྱེ་བོ་ཁོ་ནར་ནས།། ༡༡༦།།

བསྐྱེངས་དང་བྲལ་ལ་མོད་དུ་གསོལ་ཅི་འཚོལ།
ཕན་པའི་གདམས་ངག་དོན་པོ་འདི་ལགས་ཏེ།
ཁྱོད་ཀྱི་ཐུགས་དཔལ་མཛོད་ཅིག་བཅོམ་ལྡན་གྱིས།
སེམས་ནི་ཆོས་ཀྱི་རྩ་བ་ལེགས་པར་གསུངས།། ༡༡༦ །།

ཁྱོད་ལ་དེ་སྐད་གདམས་པ་གང་ལགས་དེ།
ཐས་པར་དགེ་སློང་གིས་ཀྱང་བསྒྲུ་བར་དཀའ།
འདི་ལས་གང་ཞིག་སྤྱོད་པའི་ངོ་བོ་དེའི།
ཡོན་ཏན་བསྟེན་པས་སྐུ་ཚེ་དོན་ཡོད་མཛོད།། ༡༡༧ །།

ཀུན་གྱི་དགེ་བ་ཀུན་ལ་ཡི་རང་ཞིང་།
ཉིད་ཀྱིས་ལེགས་པར་སྤྱད་པ་རྣམ་གསུམ་ཡང་།
སངས་རྒྱས་ཉིད་ཐོབ་བགྱི་སླད་ཡོངས་བསྔོས་ནས།
དེ་ནས་དགེ་བའི་ཕུང་པོ་འདི་ཡིས་ཁྱོད།། ༡༡༨ །།

སྐྱེ་བ་དཔག་ཏུ་མེད་པ་ལྷ་མི་ཡི།
འཇིག་རྟེན་ཀུན་གྱི་རྣལ་འབྱོར་དབང་མཛད་ནས།
འཕགས་པ་སྤྱན་རས་གཟིགས་དབང་སྤྱོད་པ་ཡིས།
སྐྱེ་བོ་ཉམ་ཐག་མང་པོ་རྗེས་བཟུང་སྐྱོ།། ༡༣༠ ༎

འབྲུངས་ནས་ན་རྒ་འདོད་ཆགས་ཞེ་སྡང་རྣམས།
བསལ་ཏེ་སངས་རྒྱས་ཞིང་དུ་བཅོམ་ལྡན་འདས།
འོད་དཔག་མེད་དང་འདྲ་བར་འཇིག་རྟེན་གྱི།
མགོན་པོ་སྐྱེ་ཚེ་དཔག་ཏུ་མེད་པར་མཛད།། ༡༣༡ ༎

ཤེས་རབ་ཚུལ་ཁྲིམས་གཏོང་འབྱུང་གྲགས་ཆེན་དྲི་མ་མེད།
ལྷ་ཡུལ་ནས་མཁའ་དང་ནི་ས་སྟེང་རྒྱལ་མཛད་ནས།
ས་ལ་ཟེ་དང་མཐོ་རིས་ལྷ་ནི་ན་ཀུང་མཆོག
བདེ་དགའ་དགའ་བ་ངེས་པར་རབ་ཏུ་ཞི་མཛད་དེ།། ༡༣༢ ༎

ཉོན་མོངས་ཉམ་ཐག་སེམས་ཅན་ཚོགས་ཀྱི་འཇིགས་སྐྱོ་དང་།
འཆི་བ་ཞི་མཛད་རྒྱལ་བའི་དབང་པོ་ཉིད་བརྙེས་ནས།
འཇིག་རྟེན་ལས་འདས་མིང་ཙམ་ཞི་ལ་མི་བསྙེངས་པ།
མི་བསྒྲེས་འོངས་པ་མི་མངའི་གོ་འཕང་བརྙེས་པར་མཛོད།། ༡༢༣།།

བཤེས་པའི་སྤྲིངས་ཡིག་སློབ་དཔོན་ཆེན་པོ་··
འཕགས་པ་ཀླུ་སྒྲུབ་ཀྱིས་མཛའ་བོ་བདེ་སྤྱོད་····
བཟང་པོ་ལ་བསྐུར་བ་རྫོགས་སོ།།

རྒྱ་གར་གྱི་མཁན་པོ་སརྦ་ཛྙཱ་དེ་བ་དང་ ཞུ་
ཆེན་གྱི་ལོ་ཙྪ་བ་བནྡེ་དཔལ་བརྩེགས་ཀྱིས་བསྒྱུར་
ཅིང་ཞུས་ཏེ་གཏན་ལ་ཕབ་པའོ།། ||

APPENDIX II

Glossary of some English terms used in the text with Tibetan and Sanskrit Equivalents

ENGLISH	TIBETAN	SANSKRIT
aggregate	phung.po.	skandha
anger	khro.ba.	kopa, krodha
animal	dud. 'gro.	paśu, tiryak
attachment	chags.pa., 'dod. chags.	rāga
birth	skye.ba.	jāti
Blessed One	bcom.ldan.,das.	bhagavān
body	lus.	rūpa, kāya
chance	'dod.rgyal.	yadṛcchā
common people	so.so.'i.skye.bo.	pṛthagjana
compassion	sṇying.rje.	karuṇā
concentration	bsam.gtan.	dhyāna
conqueror	rgyal.ba.	jina
consciousness	rnam.par.shes.pa.	vijñāna
contact	reg.pa.	sparśa
corrective	gnyen.po.	pratipakṣa
craving	sred.pa.	tṛṣṇā
death	'chi.ba.	maraṇa, mṛtyu
dedicate	bsngos. ba.	pariṇāmana
deed, action	las.	karma
defilement	nyon.mongs.	kleśa
demigod	lha.min.	asura
desire	'dod.pa.	kāma
discrimination of dharmas	chos.rab. 'byed.	dharmapravicaya
disease	na.	vyādhi
dissatisfaction	'dod.pas.'phongs.	kāmadaridra
doubt	the.tshom.	vicikitsā
energy	btson.('grus.)	vīrya
(the) Enlightened One	sangs.rgyas.	Buddha

enlightenment	byang. chub	bodhi
equanimity, even-mindedness	btang.snyoms.	upekṣā
existence, becoming	srid.pa.	bhava
faith	dad.pa.	śraddhā
faultless	nongs.pa.mi.mnga.	nirdoṣa
fear	'jigs.pa.	bhaya
feeling	tshọr.ba.	vedanā
form	gzugs.	rūpa
Four Noble Truths	phags.pa.'i.bden.pa bzhi.	catvāryāryasatyāni
fruit, effect, result	'bras.bu.	phalam
giving	sbyin.pa.,gtong.	dāna, tyāga
God	dbang.phyug.	īśvara
god	lha.	deva
grasping	len.pa.	upādāna
Great Sage	thub.pa.chen.po.	mahāmuni
happiness	bde.ba.	sukha
hatred	zhe.sdang.	dveṣa
heaven	mtho.ris.	svarga
heedfulness	bag.yod.	apramāda
hell	dmyal.ba.	naraka
Holy One	'phags.pa.	ārya
hungry ghost	yi.dwags.	preta
ignorance	ma.rig.pa.	avidyā
impermanent	mi.rtag.pa.	anitya
impure	mi.gtsang.ba.	aśubha, aśuci
inexpressible	lung.ma.bstan.pa.	avyākṛta
Interdependent Origination	rten.cing. 'brel. bar. 'byung.ba.	pratītyasamutpāda
irreversible stage	phyir.mi.ldog.pa.	avaivartika
joy	dga.ba.	muditā, nanda
liberation	thar.pa.	mokṣa
love	byams.pa.	maitrī
lying	brdzun.	mṛṣā
merit	bsod.nams.	puṇya
mind	sems.,yid., thugs.	citta, manaḥ
monk	dge.slong.	bhikṣu
morality	tshul.khrims.	śīla

morality and useless religious practices	tshul.khrims.brtul. zhugs.mchog.'dzin.	śīlavrataparāmarśa
name and form	ming.dang.gzugs.	nāmarūpa
nature	rang.bzhin.	prakṛti, svabhāva
Nirvāṇa	mya.ngan.las. 'das. pa.	nirvāṇa
Noble Assembly	dge. 'dun.	saṅgha
Noble Eightfold Path	'phags.pa'i.lam.yan lag.brgyad.	āryāṣṭāṅgikamārga
not happy	mi.bde.ba.	asukha
object	yul.	viṣaya
obscuration	sgrib.pa.	āvaraṇa
obstacle	gegs., bar.chad.	avarodha
old age	rga.ba.	jarā
own-being	ngo.do.nyid.	svabhāvatā
patience	bzod. pa.	kṣānti
path	lam.	mārga, patha
peace	zhi.ba.	śama, śānti
penance	dka'.thub.	tapasyā
perfection	pha.rol.tu.phyin.pa.	pāramitā
precept	bsnyen.gnas.	upavāsastha
predisposition	'du.byed., las.	saṃskāra
purification	shin.tu.sbyangs.pa.	praśuddhi
reality	de.kho.na.nyid.	tattva
realm of desire	'dod.spyod.	kāmāvacara
religion	chos.	dharma
remembrance, mindfulness	dran.pa.	smṛti
right view	yang.dag.par.lta.ba.	samyagdṛṣṭi
ripen, ripened (result)	rnam.smin.	vipāka
satisfaction	chog.shes.pa.	saṃtoṣa
seed	sa.bon.	bīja
self, soul	bdag.	ātma
selfless, soulless, devoid of self	bdag.med.	anātma, nairātmya
sense-organs (six)	skye.mched.drug	ṣaḍāyatana
sentient beings, living beings	sems.can.	sattva

sexual misconduct	'khrig.pa.	maithuna
sin	sdig.pa.	pāpa
sorrow	mya.ngan.	śoka
source	'byung.gnas.	ākara
speech, voice	ngag.	vāk
spiritual friend	dge.ba'i.bshes. gnyen.	kalyāṇamitra
state	go.'phang.	pada
stealing	chom.rkun.	caurya
study, listening	thos.pa.	śruti
suffering	sdug.bsngal.	duḥkha
(the Buddha's) teaching	chos.	dharma
time	dus.	kāla
trance	ting.nges. 'dzin.	samādhi
transcendent	'jig.rten.las. 'das. pa.	lokottara
Ultimate Truth	don.dam.bden.pa.	paramārthasatya
universal monarch	'khor.los.bsgyur. ba.	cakravartin
violence, killing	'tshe	hiṃsā
virtue	dge.ba.	kuśala
wisdom	shes.rab.	prajñā
wrong view	phyin.ci.log.par.lta. ba.	mithyādṛṣṭi

INDEX